get off the fence!

get off the fence!

MORALS FOR MODERNS

Thomas A. Fry, Jr.

FLEMING H. REVELL COMPANY

542

Scripture passages in this book, unless otherwise identified, are from the *Revised Standard Version of the Bible,* copyrighted 1946 and 1952.

This book is dedicated to my wife,
who has lead me in Faith,
supported me in serving Truth,
and shown me the meaning of Love

contents

get off the fence!

1

communism,
our great opportunity

COMMUNISM IS our archenemy. Secretary of State Dean Rusk has said, "No one has to convince us that the contest between Communist imperialism and freedom is for keeps, and nobody has to convince us that when Khrushchev said he would bury us, he was claiming not just an alleged historical inevitability, but an objective toward which Communists work relentlessly."

If communism were only our national enemy, the situation would be serious enough. But it is also our ideological and spiritual enemy. History has proven that it has no concept of justice, no place for individual freedom, no desire for peace, no sense of responsibility to moral standards, and no respect for God. Communism is the enemy of religion, of justice, of democracy, of freedom, of God; it is therefore the enemy of man's highest and noblest life and ambition.

This being so, it seems strange that an ideology which had no national following less than fifty years ago should now control over a billion people on this earth, and that it should be viewed sympathetically by so many others in Latin America, Africa, Asia, Europe, and even in the

11

United States. While it is true that communism has never been voted into power by a majority vote in a single nation, we must never forget that its appeal has been strong enough to cause one citizen of our own country to say, "The Soviet Union is the only fatherland of the workers and toilers the world over; whose major international task is to seek the defeat of the enemies of the Soviet Union." Nor was it with a gun at his back that a leader of a Latin American country said, "The people of Chile will never fight against the Soviet Union, the bulwark of peace and democracy, defender of the oppressed and dependent peoples."

Communism could never have enlisted such support without some form of appeal. If we are going to win in this ideological warfare we must understand something of that appeal.

Communism has directed its chief appeal toward dispossessed workers and farmers. Even today the American Communist Party views the years of the great depression as the golden era. Men who are willing to work but who cannot find a job become emotionally aware of the weaknesses of the system under which they are living, and are open-minded to propaganda concerning any system that claims it can solve their problems.

Surely this constitutes communism's great appeal in Latin America where farmers have worked for starvation wages for generations. These people have seen the little they have wiped out by inflation and famine while their governments and economy have been supported by American politics and American economic power. They are ready to try a new system—communism seems to be the only alternative.

12

History thus far has been on the side of the Communists. Their rise to power is so recent that the world has not yet seen clearly what their system does to the worker or the farmer. Not knowing any better, desperate people rally to the call, "Workers of the world, unite. You have nothing to lose but your chains."

Communism also makes a broad appeal to disinherited minority groups in our country and abroad. Much of its energy has been spent in trying to influence colored people. Its approach to them emphasizes the theme that in communism there are no racial barriers. Its avowed aim is to unite all the disinherited—white and black, yellow and brown—against their oppressors. The enemy is pictured as the capitalistic system; the true brotherhood is pictured as the Communist Party. The Communists have failed in the United States because, as one Negro put it, "We want more democracy, not less."

The wisdom of the average American Negro has not prevailed throughout the world. In other parts of the globe, incidents such as the one at the University of Mississippi drive the wedge deeper between the colored peoples and the democracies and push them closer to the Red orbit.

Communism has made its appeal to disillusioned idealists. Some of the world's moral and intellectual dreamers have found it impossible to work against vested interests that support injustices, police-state methods, and inequities in their society. In desperation some idealists have become advocates of revolution.

Then there is the Communists' appeal to the dismayed peacemakers. They have sold millions the idea that they offer peace to our world. Khrushchev's sword-rattling has been directed toward the United States, but to the rest of the world he has held out the olive branch. This appeals to nations that fear atomic warfare, particularly those in Latin America. Young men whose vocations might be curtailed by military service, mothers and widows who fear for their loved ones, those who feel that the tax burden is too heavy—many of these have rallied behind Khrushchev's calls to "peace." Emotions run particularly high in nations that have been made to feel that there is no purpose in any resistance but "to pull the chestnuts of the United States out of the fire."

The aims of communism within the free world are equally clear. First of all they want to foment agitation. They are not interested in finding solutions to the problems of labor, race, or war; rather, it is their purpose to create ill will, distrust, and disillusionment. They want to weaken us by internal strife.

A second objective is to create distrust in our institutions and leadership. Any time they can create distrust in our government or in a government in another part of the world, any time they can cast doubt on the activities of Wall Street or our civic leadership, they have struck a telling blow at democracy and the free-enterprise system.

Wherever we leave ourselves open to criticism we give the Communists an opportunity to discredit our democratic system. One has only to listen to Radio Moscow to learn how they seek to distort our way of life. They play up our recessions, saying that we are on the verge of economic collapse and that every city has long bread lines. They imply that racial strife is constant in all of our cities. They try to make the people of the world think we are still living in the days of the sweat shops, of police cruelty, of wanton immorality, and of child labor.

In the museum of Chapultepec in Mexico City hangs a mural depicting the struggle of the Mexican people with the Roman Catholic Church. The priests are pictured with claws instead of hands, and fangs instead of teeth. The Roman Catholic Church has not lived up to its ideals in Latin America, but its evil has been distorted beyond recognition in this mural. The viewer is not surprised to find that it was painted by a Communist. One of the ways in which they attempt to destroy an enemy is the magnification and distortion of his weaknesses.

Communism also aims to indoctrinate the world. This indoctrination is not education, for by our standards education means seeking for truth. The Communists want to rewrite history and then publicize their peculiar interpretations of it. Through pamphlets, movies, entertainment, they would win mankind.

Their ultimate aim is to foster and aid revolution. Those who doubt this need look no farther than Cuba. Our newspapers tell us of their aims at revolution in other countries. I have in my library a book entitled *The Communists Can Be Trusted*. They can indeed be trusted to work for their ultimate aim: a revolution that will destroy the free world and make of it one Communist state.

To accomplish these purposes the Communists use four techniques. First of all, they seek to infiltrate every important phase of life. They try to get their workers in key positions in labor unions, government, educational institutions, radio and television, organizations of minorities, and the churches. By getting workers in these key

15

positions they can create disturbances and distrust, incite riots, distort, propagandize, and undermine our religion and morals.

Communists have also sought to accomplish their aims through front groups created to slow down our defense efforts, to seek aid for Communist countries, and to emphasize difficulties in our own nation. Never have these front groups sought to solve problems; they magnify and publicize them. These groups have often been endorsed by well-meaning citizens who, through misguided zeal and misunderstood idealism, have helped the Communists.

The most obvious method the Communists use to accomplish their aims is direct propaganda. This has been handled by personal contacts, pamphlets, and every other possible means of communication. We do not need to dwell on the techniques of open insurrection and revolution—which have been the only means by which they have fulfilled their mission in any single country they have taken over.

It is true that we face a great danger. It is also true that communism offers Americans a great challenge. How can we meet it?

Personally I do not feel called upon to take part in any underground military organization. I firmly believe that there is enough wisdom in the Federal Bureau of Investigation and enough power in the Army of the United States to prevent any Communist attempt to overthrow our government by military force. Our basic battle is not one of guns but of the spirit. Any victory in arms would be completely unavailing if it were not preceded by, accompanied by, and followed by a victory for God and truth. It is therefore not to the political and military, but to the moral and spiritual that we must dedicate ourselves.

First of all we must dedicate ourselves to the church, to its message, its institutions, and its program. Surveys point to an appalling decrease in church attendance in our country during the past several years. If ever there was a time when we needed to get behind the worship, educational, and missionary programs of the church, it is now.

The advent of Sputnik revolutionized our schools. All the courses have been enriched and homework has been increased. These heavy demands on our students have kept more and more young people and families from attending Bible studies in churches—and at a time when we need to give to our youth the moral and spiritual guidance that only faith can give to them.

In this day of growing secularization of our society, are you seeing to it that your family learns the Bible as well as biology? Are you zealous that your young people learn and practice the Ten Commandments with the same thoroughness that they apply to the multiplication tables? Is your family part of the problem of the devaluation of our fundamental values, or is it part of the growing knowledge of the Christian faith? This problem of increased secularization can be solved only on an individual and family basis. If we are to meet the challenge of communism we must rededicate ourselves to the spiritual truths of life.

How does our giving to the church stack up when compared to our challenge? An officer in my church recently called me to talk about the number of members who are still giving two and three hundred dollars a year to the work of the church while they are living as though their incomes were in the ten-thousand-dollar-a-year-or-above bracket. Can we honestly say that we are doing our part to meet the challenge?

Need I remind you of the words of Kagawa when thirty years ago he asked us to send missionaries to Japan? He warned us that unless we sent missionaries we would send soldiers. We did not send the missionaries, but we had to send the soldiers. In this day, if we do not send the Bible to the world we will be sending our bombs.

We must also rededicate ourselves to making democracy and free enterprise work. If Washington seems corrupt it is because of the men we send there. If our state capitals seem to represent a lack of ideals it is because some voting districts send men of small character as representatives.

Americans play into Communist hands every time there is an unnecessary strike, every time a business fails, every time a stupid or unethical political leader is elected. Do you thoroughly investigate the candidates running for office? Do you work for men who will best enable us to meet the challenges of our day? If not, how can you justify your existence in a free society in these trying times?

Finally, we must dedicate ourselves to Christianity and to Christ's highest ideals. If anyone were to listen to the Communists, he would think that it is they and not we who worship the Prince of Peace. He would think that the Communists are more concerned with the moral and spiritual values than we are, and that only Communists preach justice and the worth of the individual.

He might even think that Karl Marx uttered the words, ". . . proclaim liberty throughout the land . . ." (LEVITICUS 25:10).

I am reminded of the words of Patrick Henry: "Why stand we here to idle? What is it that gentlemen wish? What would they have? Is life so dear or peace so sweet as to be purchased at the price of chains and slavery? Forbid it, Almighty God. I know not what course others may take, but as for me, give me liberty or give me death." I am also reminded of the words of André Gide: "I consider that on account of its compromises Christianity is bankrupt. I have written and I firmly believe that if Christianity had really prevailed and if it had really fulfilled the teachings of Christ there would today be no question of communism; there would indeed be no social problem at all."

Our world is divided into two warring camps and the decision does not seem to have been reached. Total war may be avoided. The power of communism can be met only by a power greater than its own; by an ethic broader than the Communist ethic; by a devotion that goes deeper than the Communist's devotion to his party. The challenge is ours. As soon as we begin to live our faith the world will see our good works and give glory to God who is in heaven.

The way before us is not yet completely black. The church still holds a flickering lamp. God help us if we fail in this, our hour of greatest opportunity.

2

what you just said

ANY SYSTEM of morals must have as one of its fundamental components the integrity of the spoken and written word. Without this there can be no successful civilization.

Joy Davidman reminds us of this in the story of a man who knew of a plot to overthrow his government. This man's conscience and love of country made him divulge all his information. The plotters he named belonged to a small, already unpopular minority who were suspected of taking orders from a foreign power. Because of that suspicion, the man's testimony found ready belief. Of course it was welcomed by politicians who had axes to grind and reputable opponents they wanted to discredit.

The man proved to have an inexhaustible memory. Each new questioning brought out new facts and new names. Government officials were not above suspicion and popular hysteria knew no bounds. People who had been known and respected for years were ferreted out by the infallible informer, stripped of their jobs and their freedom. The informer quickly gathered support from many others who added names and details. Men began to eye their closest friends with suspicion and to look for revolution in every public meeting. The frenzy lasted for several years, during which time hard-won civil liberties were cast aside, rules of evidence were forgotten, and slander was accepted as proof.

The man? One Titus Oates. The year? 1687. The conspiracy? The so-called Popish Plot which for months had English Protestants believing that their innocent Catholic neighbors were about to murder them with fire and sword. London did not deal mildly with false witnesses: when Titus Oates was convicted of his perjuries he was whipped from one end of London to the other.

The reason the story is so meaningful to us is that we fear the same thing may have happened in our own less credulous generation. We remember the Communist trials, and in more recent years the senate investigations into rackets and unions. Time has not stopped the lips of those who want to win public acclaim through perjury and slander.

Slander can go on outside the public courtroom as well as inside. When former President William Howard Taft was visiting Hampton Institute he was overheard talking to a charming woman who was also to speak at the college convocation. Handing the woman her wrap, Mr. Taft said, "Perhaps you had better carry it yourself. If we should be separated and I was found with this wrap I might be accused of having stolen it." "Why, Mr. Taft," she said laughingly, "are you accustomed to such accusations?" "My dear lady," replied President Taft, "I am accustomed to anything. I have been President of the United States."

In our courtrooms, political campaigns, bull sessions, and club meetings, in our telephone conversations, ad-

vertising, and at times in our churches, false witnessing
has become an accepted art.

In the ancient code of Hammurabi the first laws dealt
with the matter of false witnessing, and on a Babylonian
cuneiform tablet we can read this inscription:

> Slander not, but speak kindness,
> Speak not evil, but show good will;
> Whoso slanders and speaks evil
> Unto him will Shamash requite it.

A. Powell Davies points out the universality of laws
against slander when he says, "The requirements of ver-
acity, not only in preferring criminal charges, but in all
matters that could damage another person's interest or
reputation, had been upheld since the dawn of civilization. Like the three other commandments that express prohibitions elaborated in the criminal codes, it
is not Hebrew but universal. Murder, adultery, theft, and
false witness, although variously defined at different times
and in different places, have been crimes carrying severe
penalties ever since man began to make laws."

God, through the author of the Book of Deuteronomy,
indicated how seriously He takes this matter of slander
when He specified the penalty that the Hebrews were to
inflict on the guilty party: "If a malicious witness rises
against any man to accuse him of wrongdoing, then both
parties to the dispute shall appear before the Lord, before
the priests and the judges who are in office in those days;
the judges shall inquire diligently, and if the witness is
a false witness and has accused his brother falsely, then
you shall do to him as he had meant to do to his
brother; so you shall purge the evil from the midst of
you" (19:16-19).

Do you catch the import of this ancient Hebrew law? The first law of the code of Hammurabi contains a similar statement: "If a man accuse a man, and charge him with murder, and cannot convict him, the accuser shall be put to death."

The meaning of these laws is clear: if a man accuses another falsely, and his faithlessness is found out, then society shall do to that man what he had intended to do to his opponent. Surely this law would purge the evil from the midst of the land.

According to this law, a politician who falsely accuses his opponent of misusing public funds would receive the punishment society had ordained for misappropriation of funds. Such a law would take the mud out of many political speeches.

According to this law, a neighbor who falsely suggests the immorality of an acquaintance would receive the punishment society has prescribed for the moral offense. Such action would limit some backyard conversations.

According to this law, the businessman who falsely suggests that his competitor sells goods that are inferior would receive the ostracism society forces upon those who sell inferior goods. This would cut down on some of the misleading advertising.

According to this law, the ball player or spectator who accuses another player or an official of cheating would receive the punishment given to one who had "thrown" a ball game. Such laws would eliminate some rhubarbs in our games.

Slander also has eternal connotations. In writing of the new Jerusalem in the Book of Revelation, John says, ". . . nothing unclean shall enter it, nor any one who practices abomination or falsehood. . . . Outside are the dogs and sorcerers and fornicators and murderers and idolaters, and every one who loves and practices falsehood" (21:27; 22:15). Certainly a practice so universally denounced—one that causes God to suggest such stringent punishment and one with such eternal significance—should be considered most seriously.

Why has false witnessing been universally denounced? Some might suspect that the indictments have come from professional religionists and lawmakers who really do not understand human nature. After all, a man has to get elected to office and sometimes the only way he can do it is to make the voters distrust his opponent. And then, too, all of the telephone gossip is not meant seriously. What fun is there in talking if you can't discuss people? No one is interested in Mrs. Jones' operation, but everyone is interested in Mrs. Jones' daughter's courtship. Why take a bit of political talk and gossip so seriously?

First of all, the social order is disrupted by false witnesses. All social order must have integrity as the foundation of its legal, legislative, judicial, and economic systems. Justice in the courts can be paralyzed by those who do not tell the truth. Our banks would be destroyed in a moment if people's words had no value.

I am more and more impressed with these facts as I read of the trials behind the Iron Curtain. Robert Vogeler's book *I Was Stalin's Prisoner* is not only horrible in its description of the treatment Vogeler received from the Communists; it is even more terrifying in its insights into their judicial system. Vogeler was finally coerced into swearing to things that both he and the court knew he had never done. The state then produced other false witnesses to testify with Vogeler on false charges.

24

False witnessing can destroy man's most generous impulses. Dr. Clovis Chappell tells of a minister who had been called upon by a number of men seeking charity. Quite obviously most of them only wanted money to get something to drink. Finally the parson found that both his patience and his pocketbook were thin. He turned the last man away hurriedly. Two days later the man's body was found not far from the parsonage and an autopsy showed that he had died of starvation. The parson began to look upon himself as a murderer, but actually the murderers were the men who had lied to him so often about being hungry that he did not believe an honest man when he came to the door.

False witnessing also destroys the lives and the livelihoods of those who have been falsely accused. Our Lord was put on the cross by men who bore false witness against Him. How many of our political leaders have lost campaigns and reputations because some people manufactured pictures that made them seem to be friendly with left-wing leaders, or falsely represented them as a front for an organization unpopular with the electorate? How many men have lost their jobs because someone suggested that they were not supporting the company's policy? How many homes have been broken by lies spread by supposedly honorable people?

Shakespeare pointed to the value of a good name when he said (*Othello*):

> Good name in man and woman, dear my lord,
> Is the immediate jewel of our souls:
> Who steals my purse steals trash; . . .
> But he that filches from me my good name

542

Robs me of that which not enriches him
And makes me poor indeed.

The writer of Proverbs (6:16-19) indicates God's feeling about gossip when he says: "There are six things
which the Lord hates, seven which are an abomination
to him: haughty eyes, a lying tongue, and hands that
shed innocent blood, a heart that devises wicked plans,
feet that make haste to run to evil, a false witness who
breathes out lies, and a man who sows discord among
brothers."

James describes the sin a bit more picturesquely: ". . .
the tongue is a fire. The tongue is an unrighteous world
among our members, staining the whole body, setting on
fire the cycle of nature, and set on fire by hell. . . .
the tongue—a restless evil, full of deadly poison"
(3:6, 8).

These words are a warning to those who sometimes
wonder whether they have become fault-finders and false
witnesses. Interestingly enough, fault-finders are often
false witnesses. They do not mean to be, but when their
criticisms are analyzed they are usually only half-truths or
dishonest questionings.

Dr. Julian Lake reported the findings of two physicians who made a study of tensions based on thousands
of cases. The doctors set up two groups: in the first
group were people who were unable to relax, and in
the second group were those who were relatively free
from tension. They discovered that the tense people had
one thing in common which was not prevalent among
the relaxed group—they were all extremely critical of
others. When those in the tense group began to find ways

of saying nice things about people they overcame their tenseness.

Dr. Lake also described the case of a girl with whom he worked. As a young girl she had had few friends because her schoolmates were afraid of her sharp tongue. Her family tried to help her but were unsuccessful because of her critical attitude toward them. Finally the girl left school and took a job in an office, but things did not go well there. She did not feel she could trust her office associates, nor did they like her. The girl was very affectionate, but could not find anyone who would date her more than one or two times. Finally a man did come along who seemingly understood her and paid little attention to her critical tongue. They were married and at last her problem seemed to be solved. But the critical attitude that had not bothered her husband during their courtship became unbearable in their home. Finally the marriage came to the verge of divorce. The girl went to a psychiatrist to see whether he could help the home situation. After lengthy talks with her and her husband, the psychiatrist had but one suggestion for her: "You must get rid of your spirit of fault-finding."

Every minister wishes that he could say that word personally to many embittered people in his congregation. The person who is not happy in one office, in one marriage, or in one church, will not be happy in another. These people soon make a name for themselves. People come to know that no friendship with them will last. Eventually every acquaintance who becomes a friend is discarded. Critics have to live in a world alone because they trust no one, love no one, get along with no one. They are living, but inside they are dead—not only dead in this life but dead eternally, for the Bible says that no one who "loves and practices falsehood" shall enter the Kingdom of God. The God who concerns Himself with the hairs on a man's head also concerns Himself with the shreds of a man's reputation.

Anything as serious as this should make all of us ask, "Is it I, Lord?" (Matthew 26:22). We would do well to investigate some of the recognized techniques of false witnessing.

First, there is the technique of the absolute lie. Have you ever called a woman a gold digger or a cradle snatcher or a grave digger? Perhaps you have called a doctor a quack or a lawyer a dunce. If you have, you might remind yourself that even the courts of our land have ruled that such words constitute slander if you cannot actually prove your statements.

Of course you may say that you did not really mean it, but did you say that you did not mean it to the one to whom you were talking? The writer of Proverbs has a comment about those who claim they were only joking: "Like a madman who throws firebrands, arrows, and death, is the man who deceives his neighbor and says, 'I am only joking!'" (26:18, 19).

We can get into habits of running people down until we hardly recognize what we are doing. Have you ever heard anyone say, "He doesn't know the truth when he sees it"? That is an absolute lie that someone is telling about another person. Have you ever said about a man, "I know that he knows about the corruption in his office"? Can you prove that he knows about the corruption or are you only making an inference from what you have heard? We wonder whether people who say of someone

28

else, "He is as crooked as a corkscrew," would like to prove that statement in court.

Unless you have the facts and can prove them, you are bearing false witness against your neighbor when you make careless accusations. If you do have facts and actually can prove the things that you say, then as a good citizen you should prove your accusations and remove another evil from our land.

We can even bear false witness through the use of truth. A friend of mine in Washington was smeared and almost ruined by a newspaper columnist who reported that he had never seen this man without a drink in his hand. Every time the columnist saw this man at a gathering he made the same report. The report was true, but the inferences drawn from the true statement were definitely false. This political leader attended many social gatherings as a representative of one of our highest officials. He had found that the best way to handle the drinking problem was to take a cocktail when he entered, hold the full glass through the evening, and then deposit it as he left the party. In that way he was not constantly harassed by people urging him to have a drink. True, the reporter had never seen him without a drink in his hand, but the reporter had never seen the man swallow the drink. What he reported was true, but the inference was a false witness, a black lie.

The half-truth is one of the most widely used techniques for bearing false witness. Jesus' statement that He would destroy the temple and rebuild it in three days was taken out of its context and He was killed for saying it. Enemies took His statement that He was a King and used it to put pressure on Pilate to murder Him.

A certain minister was once asked to lead a prayer of thanksgiving for the accomplishments of a fellow minister. In his prayer the minister used this sentence: "We thank God for the work that this fellow minister has done, or is alleged to have done." Now he was absolutely honest: he had never seen the results of the other minister's work; all he knew was what had been told him. But by using the words "or is alleged to have done" in his prayer, he created a doubt in the minds of his listeners. If you say, "He is reported to have done a good job," or "I guess some people like him," you are thereby creating an atmosphere of suspicion and thus bearing false witness, even though you are not violating the truth.

In the Book of Job there is a form of false witnessing through questions. In the councils of heaven God was discussing people on earth. He happened to mention Job and said that he was a just and upright man, one who feared God and turned his back on evil. Satan could not challenge this statement, but he raised a question: " 'Does Job fear God for nought?' " (1:9).

One question such as, "Was he drinking when the accident happened?" or "Was that the only reason he lost his job?" or "How long after the marriage did the baby come?" may be just enough to create a false impression in the minds of those who are listening. In asking such questions you have not told a lie but you have certainly borne false witness.

Finally, there is the false witness of faint praise. Dr. Elton Trueblood describes the way this is carried on in academic circles: "If we wish to suggest that a man's scholarship is superficial rather than deep, we point out his adeptness at popularization. Equally damaging is

30

3

handling hard decisions

DECISIONS ARE problems for all of us. We wonder what to do about drinking or about requiring our children to come home at a certain hour. We wonder about the morality of some business transactions, wages, and advertisements. We will be able to deal more effectively with decisions if we follow a few guides.

Our consciences can be powerful instruments for keeping us on the right track in life. Conscience kept the father of Channing Pollock faithful to his duty when yellow fever was causing scores of deaths every day in San Salvador. He was in the United States diplomatic service and when the plague struck he had already planned to leave for his vacation back home. His family begged him to come home, but he wrote: "I do not think any responsible officer should be away at a time like this. Our people are frightened and confused. Some of them have been refused Christian burial. It is my job to stay here and look after them." Later on he was asked, "Have you no fear?" His reply was, "None as great as the fear of not doing what I believe to be right."

While conscience can be a power to strengthen a man's action, the content of a conscience is not given by God. Natives in some cannibalistic tribes believe that they

will sin if they do not eat the bodies of their dead opponents. Some primitive societies feel a strict moral obligation to bury alive the widow of a deceased man. Not
many years ago it was deemed right for a man to own
slaves but it was immoral for him to play cards or dance.
There are some parents today who feel guilty if they
allow their daughters to wear lipstick.

We can say that conscience is like a very fine watch—
it is a mechanism given us by God to guide us in our
morality. The accuracy of a watch depends not only on
its inner works but on the accuracy with which it is set
and the constancy with which it is kept wound. If a man
drives from one time zone to another and forgets to
change the setting of his watch, it will not give him the
right time.

Our consciences are not set by God but by our culture,
environment, parents, and friends. We grow up with an
emotional power to continue to do what we were taught
in childhood and youth. If we were taught wrong, then
our consciences direct us in the wrong paths.

Another way in which our consciences can lead us
astray is most effectively illustrated by a story. Wilfred
Grenfell had just received a new boat for his work in Lab-
rador. He received a call one night from a sick woman
who asked him to help her. Accompanied by several companions, he started off in the boat. After traveling some
distance they discovered they were going in the wrong
direction and in order to save their lives it was necessary
to run the boat aground. Grenfell never got to the sick
woman; she died, and Grenfell almost lost his life.

An investigation showed that the workman in Liver-
pool who had been assigned to assemble the boat had

dropped the brass screw used to attach the compass. Instead of finding the screw he picked up another one— a steel screw—and used it on the compass. This steel screw exerted enough magnetic force on the compass to throw the boat completely off course.

Our consciences are like compasses. Even though they may have been set correctly in youth, a powerful magnetic force can throw them off the right direction. It is so easy to justify certain behavior when we are in love, or when money is involved. Surely you have heard of the minister who got a call to a church that payed a larger salary. When his son was asked what his father was going to do about the call, he replied that his father was upstairs praying, but his mother was downstairs packing. When money, ambition, sex, hatred, or other powerful forces are put close to the conscience, it is like placing a tremendous piece of steel close to a compass.

In writing to Timothy Paul said, "This charge I commit to you, Timothy, my son, in accordance with the prophetic utterances which pointed to you, that inspired by them you may wage the good warfare, holding faith and a good conscience. By rejecting conscience, certain persons have made shipwreck of their faith . . ." (I, 1:18-19).

Admitting that conscience is far better as a power of righteousness than as a guide to righteousness, we are still confronted with the question of what principles should guide us in making the hard decisions of life. I Corinthians suggests a threefold test for making our decisions. The first part is the personal test: "What will this course of action do to me?" This question is suggested by several statements: "'All things are lawful for me,' but not all things are helpful. 'All things are lawful for me,' but I will not

37

be enslaved by anything. . . . 'All things are lawful,' but not all things build up" (6:12; 10:23). One of our translators throws an interesting light on these verses by translating the first: "I may do anything I please, but not everything I want to do is good for me."

Someone commented that life is not worth living because everything worthwhile is either immoral, illegal, or fattening. Now this statement is not so much a sad commentary on life as it is on the man who uttered it. Apparently he has learned to like only those things which are obviously bad for him.

Any moral or practical decision must be made on the basis of its effect on your life. Is it good for your health, your character, your emotional life, your future? To approve of an action because it hurts no one but yourself is to deny the fundamental Christian stewardship. You have nothing for which you are more responsible to God than yourself. How different is the attitude, "I am hurting only myself," from that of Paul when he said, "I beseech you . . . , by the mercies of God, that ye present your bodies a living sacrifice . . ." (ROMANS 12:1, KJV).

We need to ask not only whether a certain course of action is good or bad for us, but whether it has the power to enslave. Speaking of his sinful life, Dmitri (*The Brothers Karamazov*) says, "I can't help it, though I hate myself for it. That is just what made me wretched all my life, that I yearned to be honorable, yet I have always done filthy things."

We must apply another question to our decision: "Will it build character?" Society has found that many things which do not come within the scope of the Ten Commandments are destructive of character. Take for example the matter of lotteries and other forms of gambling.

In the early days of our country, some churches founded a number of small colleges that have grown to be great universities today. It is interesting to note that the churches raised money for most of these institutions through lotteries. But during the nineteenth century the businessmen of our nation found that lotteries were destroying the ambitions of laboring men, undermining the police system, and destroying character and morals. Lotteries were therefore prohibited.

Before James Garfield became President of the United States, he served for a number of years in Congress as representative of an Ohio district. One day, as he reviewed his political career, he said, "I have for many years represented a district whose approbation I greatly desired; but, though it may seem a little egotistical to say it, I desired still more approbation of one person, and his name is Garfield. He is the only man I am compelled to sleep with and eat with and live with and die with; and if I do not have his approbation I should have bad companionship."

The second part of the test to be applied in dealing with hard decisions is social. As Paul points out, "Let no one seek his own good, but the good of his neighbor" (1 CORINTHIANS 10:24). In this same connection he says, ". . . take heed lest by any means this liberty of yours become a stumblingblock to them that are weak" (1 CORINTHIANS 8:9, KJV). Jesus Himself told us, ". . . whoever causes one of these little ones who believe in me to sin, it would be better for him to have a millstone fastened round his neck, and to be drowned in the depth of the sea" (MATTHEW 18:6). Each decision must be made in terms of the effect it will have on others.

In an article in *The Atlantic Monthly* Albert Schweitzer

reminds us of the solidarity of life. But he says, "For the primitive man the circle of solidarity is limited to those whom he can look upon as his blood relatives—that is to say, the members of his tribe, who are to him his family. . . . In my hospital I have primitives. When I happen to ask a hospitalized tribesman, who is not himself bedridden, to render little services to a bedridden patient, he will consent only if the latter belongs to his tribe. If not, he will answer me candidly, 'This is no brother for me,' and neither attempts to persuade him nor threats will make him do this favor for a stranger." Schweitzer goes on to show how ethics evolve as man recognizes his moral responsibility to an ever-widening group of people.

Because each of us is an integral part of a moving world we should also give thought to the effects of our actions on future generations. A girl has no right to marry and have children by a man who is so rigid or so emotionally unbalanced as to destroy the emotional lives of their children. We have no right to bring children into the world if we cannot expect to give them a reasonable chance for a full life. Too often marriage is based upon the drives of the people involved, and it becomes an act of irresponsibility because no thought or care is given to the kind of children who will be produced by that union.

Walter Rauschenbusch has written a prayer that expresses our responsibility very well:

> Grant them sober eyes to look beyond these joyous
>   days
> To the generations yet to come, and to realize that
>   the

40

Home they build will be part of the sacred tissue of
The body of humanity, in which Thou art to dwell,
That thus they may reverence themselves and drink
    of
The cup of joy with soberness.

The social part of the test involves a consideration of those who have lived in the past. Having recited a list of the great figures of the Old Testament—Moses, Abraham, Elijah, and others—the writer of the Letter to the Hebrews says, ". . . these . . . received not the promise: God having provided some better thing for us, that they without us should not be made perfect. Wherefore seeing we also are compassed about with so great a cloud of witnesses, let us lay aside every weight, and the sin which doth so easily beset us . . ." (11:39-12:1, KJV).

There is a story about a baseball star whose blind father attended every game just to hear the crowd shout its approval of his son. The father died, and on the day after he was buried the son played the finest game of his career. When it was over he asked one of the coaches, "Did I play well?" The coach replied, "It was the best game you ever played. Why do you ask?" "Because it was the first game my father ever saw," the young man said.

The generations which have gone before us have handed a heritage on to us. They cannot achieve their full reward until we bring their sacrifices to a worthy completion.

Some people make their ethical decisions on the bases of mental, emotional, physical, and social health only. But I feel that we must go one final step and ask, "What would God have me to do?" In seeking to find the answer

41

there are two sources of information: the Ten Commandments and the life of Christ.

In its early days the machine that delivers ice at the roadside was very complicated. There were four different slots in which to put money and four different levers which could be pulled. Careful instructions were posted over the money slots but one company had so much trouble that it finally had a big sign printed and posted at eye level: "When all else fails, try reading instructions."

It is time for all of us to stop and read God's instructions for our moral behavior. The ninth commandment reads, "Thou shalt not bear false witness . . ." (EXODUS 20:16, KJV), and yet one of the temptations of some speakers is to leave false impressions in order to shock, convince, or win support. Many businesses seek to give the impression through advertising that everybody is talking about their product while half the people have never heard of it.

What about the commandment, "Thou shalt not commit adultery" (EXODUS 20:14, KJV)? There seems to be a feeling that if everyone else is doing it, then adultery has lost some of its stigma. Some people feel that as long as they love each other, then adultery can be committed without sin. There are people who feel that adultery is right because the desire is so strong. It is at this point that reliance on conscience is very dangerous. The tremendous power of our emotions can so influence our consciences that we may rationalize our actions to the point that black is white and white is black.

We must also ask what Christ would have us do. His will can be best understood by those who have made a habit of reading the gospels. For many people Christ is nothing but their culture or conscience. But He was actually a Man who walked the roads of Galilee and Jerusalem. If we want to know how to handle problems today, we can learn from Him. As Paul says, "Be imitators of me, as I am of Christ" (I CORINTHIANS 11:1).

Suzie Parker died as a missionary to China. She had heard the call to go there to work with Dr. Hudson Taylor. It was a real struggle for her father to agree to let her go, but he made the decision and explained it in this way: "All I can say is, I have nothing too precious for Jesus."

After a few months in China, Suzie Parker fell victim to typhoid fever and died. In reply to the letter in which Dr. Taylor described her useful life and glorious death, her father wrote, "In the midst of my heartbreaking grief and desolation I can truly repeat what I said when my daughter went away, 'I have nothing too precious for Jesus.'"

Every individual and every generation has particular problems. We have our problems of drinking, eating, recreation, what to read, what to watch, what to do. So many of them can be solved without going any further than asking what they will do for us. If we find that they will hurt us rather than help us, destroy character rather than build it, enslave us rather than free us, then we must turn our backs on these things.

But some of our problems are not simple. Problems such as integrated schools or segregated schools, whom to marry, what vocation to follow, how to behave on a date—these must be answered at the second level which considers the effect of the decision on all those around

43

us, on those who have gone before, and on those who are yet to come.

Some of our problems we do not understand, and they must be solved at a still higher level. These decisions must be made according to the will of God as revealed through the Ten Commandments and the life of our Lord Jesus Christ.

Dr. Douglas Steere tells of a conversation in Sweden between a young Christian and a man who was antagonistic to Christ. The opponent of our faith was asked if he disagreed with Christianity because it worked for peace and justice in the world. When the answer was "no" he was then asked if he opposed Christianity because it preached brotherhood. Again there was a negative answer and then the man thought for a moment. "I guess," he said, "what I resent in Christians is not that they are Christians but that they are not Christian enough."

4

why shouldn't we?

"*I CAN UNDERSTAND* why God gave the commandment concerning adultery, but times have changed since then. Science has perfected new techniques that prevent disease and reproduction. Why shouldn't we go the limit?"

That was an honest question. If the church is not prepared to answer with as much honesty, then we must share with the peddlers of pornography the responsibility for the moral breakdown of our day. It is not enough for Christians to decry the moral ignorance or amoral nature of a person who poses such a question. If there is no honest answer, we should admit it. If there is, we should give reasons for our convictions without defensiveness or arrogance.

The young man who asked the question realizes that one must deal with human emotions in a responsible manner. He understands that bringing babies into the world when there is no marriage relationship between the parents is irresponsible and unchristian. But, given the condition of a foolproof method of birth control, can he not enjoy the normal function of his body?

This young man has been misinformed. In spite of the most modern techniques, increasing numbers of lives are conceived out of wedlock, and venereal disease is spreading at an alarming rate. Every high-school class is aware of the number of its members involved in hasty marriages that produced "premature" babies. Students of marriage are aware of the number of couples who plan to wait for two years after their marriage before having their first child—only to have one after they have been married for a year. Since 1938, the number of births per thousand unmarried white women has doubled. One authority states that one out of six brides is pregnant at the time of her marriage. No, modern science has not removed the danger.

In order to deal with our contemporary problem we must understand the nature of the desire that is felt. Only those who are ignorant of or indifferent to the forces of emotional, spiritual, or social health would suggest a casual attitude toward sex.

Much of the sexual appetite does not originate in the body. I have counseled with many women who have engaged in premarital or extramarital affairs, and not a single one has ever suggested that the basic reason was physical. In practically every case their acquiescence resulted from loneliness or the desire to be accepted. Time and time again they have said, "All I really wanted was to be popular," or "to have some dates," or "for him to love me."

This is dramatically illustrated by a survey made by the Department of Health in San Francisco. Two thousand girls of proven promiscuity were given psychiatric examinations in an effort to prepare them for rehabilitation. Of these two thousand, less than one third indicated that sex gave them "some pleasure." Most of them had

46

become involved because of their loneliness or craving for acceptance. The sexual experiences were so surrounded by "doubt, guilt, and shame" that many of the girls said they were "definitely unpleasant."

Some people become involved in affairs because of resentments against parents or marital partners. People who are emotionally adolescent react strongly against the restrictions and frustrations of life. Where these reactions are deep the individual frequently lashes out against the ethics of society or the ties of the family. This attitude was expressed by one man who said, "I did it because I wanted to be free."

We all feel a need to prove ourselves to be adult men and women, and for many people adulthood is proven most vividly by sexual experience and conquest. Society adds to this misunderstanding by impressing upon us the idea that if the sexual urge is not satisfied, life has not been fulfilled.

Thus sex takes its place with alcohol and narcotics as a means of attempting to satisfy our needs for acceptance, freedom, and confidence. But, like alcohol and dope, its effects are not permanent: each mood of loneliness, frustration, or inadequacy must be met by new experiences, each of which satisfies less than similar previous experiences. Addiction to sex, like addiction to alcohol, frequently follows.

If sex apart from marriage could satisfy the inner needs to be accepted, to be free, or to have confidence, then the positive values thus accrued might possibly balance the ill effects. But experience indicates that sex without marriage does not really satisfy these needs.

Dr. Louis Bisch tells the story of a woman who came

to him for psychiatric help. She had been raised in a very restrictive home. In her early twenties she had won her liberation and had overcompensated for her past. She reported, "This new lease on life . . . went to my head. It was like gulping down champagne . . . in no time sex meant nothing. I went from one party to another, flirted, went the limit . . . then, all of a sudden, I got deathly sick of the whole thing. I had had my fling. I became so disgusted I even thought of suicide. . . . With the people I met love didn't seem to exist at all. They seldom talked about it and then only with derision. Their interests were all of the flesh. Thy talked mostly in terms of going places, drinking, meeting new bed partners . . . all of these people were completely fed up with their loose living, their frantic pursuit of pleasure. They realized it was getting them nowhere. The girls knew they were not respected by the men and that no one would ever propose marriage. Deep down, they felt that they had been wasting their time, doing what they thought everybody else was doing. They wanted so much to belong. It was pitiful."

Dr. Bisch concluded that for those who treat sex as an animal drive, sex is a swindle. Instead of giving a girl a sense of belonging and of being loved for herself, it gives her a sense of guilt. She feels that she has been used and that she has broken the laws of God and man. She is constantly afraid of pregnancy. She is ashamed of being less than the fine woman she could have been.

Sex is also a swindle for those who use it as a means of gaining self-confidence. Such confidence can be maintained only by new and more glamorous conquests. It is a confidence that can be wrecked by any decent girl who says "No." The man who seeks self-confidence in this way

48

soon realizes that he has lost his chance of being a good husband, a responsible father, a church or community leader. When confidence is gone, despair is the result.

Surely no one would suggest that sex is an adequate means of meeting the problem of resentment toward parents or marital partners. It only drives deeper the wedge of separation because guilt separates us from our loved ones. Their knowledge of our action makes trust impossible and the reconciliation that was once difficult is now rendered impossible.

When a couple get married because of pregnancy they seldom finish their academic preparation for life. Parents and part-time jobs may keep them in school for one or two years, but soon the old desires for independence from parents and for the things that a larger paycheck could afford cause them to drop out of school. The rebellion that pushes a young man into premarital sex relations drives him into rebellion against being dependent on his family for food, clothing, and shelter. If he leaves school, the rest of his life will be spent in wondering what he could have been if he had not been "trapped" by a girl and a baby. Early marriage caused by pregnancy is as poor a risk as trying to fly a small plane over Antarctica.

When we realize that the desire for intimacy is not an isolated emotion, then we can understand that sex in itself is not as strong a drive as modern culture pictures it to be. It becomes overpowering only when it is associated with a craving for acceptance, freedom, and confidence. Much of its power comes from the stimuli fed into the mind, nourished by the imagination, and triggered by the situation.

Sex was intended by God as a part of marriage. It is

49

valid for the married couple even if the marriage has been arranged by their families and they have never met before the wedding. Within the bonds of marriage it can be experienced without guilt, fear, or shame. Under such circumstances it can feed and be fed by love. It can be the expression of man's deepest appreciation instead of his resentment. It can be a source of his pride as the marriage produces children whose presence bless the home. It becomes the cement of a spiritual union. All of this can be destroyed or dissipated by premarital or extramarital sexual experience.

And so when a boy or girl asks if modern science does not make the seventh commandment obsolete, we have to reply that even a perfect contraceptive would not change this law given by God. Those who keep their sex relations within their marriage find one of God's greatest blessings to human beings. Those who engage in sexual affairs outside of marriage find one of life's most disappointing and destructive forces.

In the light of these truths there are certain suggestions that should be passed on to those who are not yet married:

1. Set high moral and spiritual goals for yourselves. The boy or girl who is determined to save the sexual experience for a marital partner is likely to get through the trials of teen-aged romance without a scar. But one who has not set this high goal is likely to fall into the trap of premarital sex.

2. Never compromise that high moral standard. Once you do, the same set of circumstances that brought about the first compromise can bring about successive deviations. Before you have succumbed

the first time, you can base your resistance to temptation on the knowledge that you are pure and wish to stay that way. There will not be this incentive after one compromise.

3. Stay away from stimulating situations; the Bible says that we should flee temptation. I am not suggesting that young people should avoid dating, but that they should avoid dating under circumstances and with persons likely to lead to trouble. I know one football coach who takes away a boy's athletic scholarship if he joins a certain campus fraternity because the fraternity has a reputation for ruining its members. The coach feels that it is safer to avoid all contact with it.

4. Keep sex and drink separated. There are signs that say, "If you drive, don't drink." Dating and drinking are as dangerous to teen-agers as driving and drinking. Drinking lowers resistance to temptation and destroys the finer sensitivities. A boy who wants to seduce a girl usually feels that the first step is to get her to take a few drinks.

5. Find constructive means of satisfying your desire for acceptance and confidence. Meet your antagonisms with adults in a way that will develop better relationships and will not destroy what good may be left in the relationship. Be part of the answer to your family's problem, and not part of the problem.

6. Establish friendships that will be allies to your high moral purposes. Not all young people in the church are pure, nor are all young people who are outside the church lacking in high moral standards. But the companions who will support Christian dedi-

51

cations are far more likely to be found in the church than in the tavern.

7. Maintain a regular and vital devotional life. Nothing affords higher idealism or a more practical deterrent power than knowing Jesus Christ and feeling His presence with you at all times.

The Old Testament gives us a commandment: "You shall not commit adultery" (EXODUS 20:14). The New Testament confronts us with an imperative: "I appeal to you therefore, brethren, by the mercies of God, to present your bodies as a living sacrifice, holy and acceptable to God, which is your spiritual worship" (ROMANS 12:1).

5

have a drink?

A DRUNK was walking down the street and noticed an electrically lighted signboard flashing its message to all who would watch it. He stared at it for a minute and then mumbled, "It can't be done." He kept saying to himself, "It can't be done. It can't be done." People gathered around him, looking at him, trying to figure out what he meant. Finally he pointed to the billboard which read, "Drink Canada Dry."

Now whether or not we wish to drink Canada dry, the problem of drinking is relevant to each one of us. Young people face the problem of whether or not they should drink. Some families have the problem of whether or not they should serve alcoholic beverages in the home. Practically all of us have a member of our family whose drinking is a serious embarrassment to us.

Drinking is not only a personal problem. It is a social problem when alcohol is a contributing cause of twenty per cent of all automobile accident deaths. Our automobile accident bill, where drinking is involved, is over a billion dollars annually. Seventy per cent of those who occupy our jails are there because of drinking problems. A large percentage of our crime bill is attributable to alcohol.

Before we seek to deal with the problem of drinking we should ask ourselves why people drink. Probably one of the main reasons is excitement. Some of us will do almost anything for excitement; it is the impulse that makes some people drive ninety miles an hour. Drinking is said to remove part of our inhibitions and leads to an exciting evening.

Some people drink to assert their independence. The moral code of society is a burden to them and they feel that they can prove their individuality and independence if they drink. This is particularly true of young people who are raised in strict, rigid homes. This type of drinking falls into the same category as does smoking for the twelve-year-old boy.

Another reason for drinking is the desire for sociability. Lots of people think drinking frees them from self-consciousness, allows emotional expression, and gives spontaneity to their conversation. By removing the veneer which our culture has spread around us, we are supposed to be more sociable. Drinking does not really enhance sociability; it just makes us more easily satisfied.

Closely associated with this is the desire to be socially acceptable. While a person may, with social grace, refuse to drink coffee, the inner sense of guilt and inferiority of people who drink often makes them reject anyone who refuses alcohol. To be socially acceptable some people will drink with the crowd.

The desire for relaxation is a primary reason for the increased amount of drinking in certain segments of our society. In our tense culture we need relaxation. But perhaps the most prevalent reason for drinking is the desire for escape. Intoxicating beverages furnish the easiest means ever discovered for escaping reality. Under the influence of alcohol a man can forget the unpaid bills, the unresponsive family, the belligerent boss. He can escape from a real or fancied slavery into a dream world where he is a fine craftsman, the complete master of home and business, an enchanting Casanova. This nightly or weekly escape from reality is for many their most precious possession. Dr. E. Stanley Jones was describing such a man when he said, "Remember, drinking is a weakness. Every time you take a drink you are a lame duck leaning on a crutch."

In the light of all these reasons, why do so many of our churches oppose the use of alcohol? It is frequently stated that the church opposes alcohol because of Biblical texts. Often quoted is I Corinthians 6:9-10: "Do not be deceived; neither the immoral, nor idolaters, nor adulterers, nor homosexuals, nor thieves, nor the greedy, nor drunkards, . . . will inherit the kingdom of God." While such passages as this can be multiplied time and time again, the church must face the fact that this text deals with drunkenness and not social drinking, and the further fact that not all Biblical texts are on the side of total abstinence.

The communion service, the most sacred of Christian ceremonies, was instituted with wine. It is well known that the first miracle our Lord performed was that of turning water into wine so that there might be enough wine for the enjoyment of a wedding party. Our Lord was condemned by the religious leaders of the day as being a "winebibber"; now if this drinking was unfermented grape juice, there would have been no reason for condemnation. Paul, the great Apostle, advocated a "little wine" to Timothy (I TIMOTHY 5:23). This was for "his stomach's sake," which gives weight to the idea that wine was prescribed for medicinal use.

When one contrasts New Testament usage of wine with the text, "Wine is a mocker, strong drink a brawler; and whoever is led astray by it is not wise" (PROVERBS 20:1), then one realizes the difficulty of making a consistent case, on Biblical grounds, for or against social drinking.

Churches do not oppose drinking now simply because they have always opposed it. St. Augustine repudiated the practice of the Aquarians who refused to drink wine. He defended its use on the ground that wine was one of the gifts of God to man. Luther and Calvin drank and extolled the virtues of drink.

It is evident that a change has taken place during more recent years which has definitely affected the thought of the church and its leadership. Churches that are closely tied with the customs of Europe are more liberal in their views about alcohol, and those that are closely tied with the United States are more vocal in their opposition to it.

What are the reasons for this change of attitude on the part of the church? One reason is the changed nature of alcoholic drinks. Although the process of distillation was known in ancient Greece and Egypt, the drinking of distilled liquors did not begin until about four hundred years ago. Until that time heavy drinking had been the luxury of the few in the wealthy classes because the fermented fruits used prior to that time made drunkenness difficult and expensive.

We have moved from an agrarian to an industrial

society. The farmer who had only to plow, plant, and cultivate could drink with his meals without any noticeable effect on the standards of his work. With the dawn of the industrial society, drinking became a problem. For men who work with a machine where split-second accuracy is demanded, drinking becomes a menace. Before the industrial revolution, farmers frequently gave their farm hands alcohol as part of their payment and even served it in the fields. Since the early days of the industrial revolution, drinking has been such a danger that a man who drinks on the job has to be replaced.

A change has also taken place in our means of transportation. It used to be that a farmer could come to town on Saturday, get drunk, and his friends would put him in his wagon and start the horses on the way home. Usually they would get home and the farmer's wife would unload her husband from the wagon, put him to bed, and all would be well. But today that same farmer comes to town, has a few drinks, and becomes a menace to the lives and limbs of all society. When he starts toward home he drives an automobile with over 150 horsepower over roads where one must be at his best. Actually the drunk is not the serious road problem today; our most serious road problem is the man who has drunk just enough to make him think he is a better driver than he really is. Twenty per cent of the automobile accidents involving the deaths of one or more people are the results of drivers who have had a drink or two.

Lest we minimize the danger of light drinking, we should remember that two bottles of beer decrease our reaction time in driving a car by one hundred per cent. Recent studies by the National Safety Council show that if a driver has had the equivalent of two cocktails his risk is increased by a ratio of five to one; if, in an evening, he has had the equivalent of five or six cocktails, his chances of having an accident are increased by more than fifty times. The same authority estimates that alcohol is involved in more than forty per cent of all traffic accidents in America.

Many in the church have come to oppose alcohol because of what it is doing to people's health. It has become a major health problem in our nation. One of our magazines says that alcohol is the greatest single cause of insanity in the United States.

There is opposition to drinking because of what it does to the morals of people. Alcohol works first on the higher brain centers, those controlling skilled performance, courtesy, moral and spiritual values and restraints. Growing up is the process of developing from the undisciplined, inexperienced child to the disciplined, discriminating adult. Drinking reverses the process and turns an adult into an undisciplined, undiscriminating child.

In a magazine story on drinking there was a questionnaire entitled "What Do You Know About It?"—meaning, What do you know about moderate drinking? The first question was, "Can a girl drink and remain virtuous?" The answer was an unequivocal "No!"

Still another reason for warning people about drinking is its effect on their futures. A fraternity with sixty boys who drink will find—if it follows the national average—that seven of those sixty will become problem drinkers during their lives and at least four will become alcoholics.

58

The director of the crime laboratory of Columbus, Ohio, states that fifty per cent of those accused of rape and crimes of passion had been drinking at the time of the crime. Eighty-three per cent of those arrested for murder had been drinking. Of those arrested for assault and for carrying a concealed weapon, ninety-two per cent had been drinking; and for larceny, burglary, and robbery, seventy to seventy-three per cent had been drinking.

It is interesting to note that of those arrested for crimes of trickery, such as forgery, only a small percentage had been drinking, and they had smaller concentrations of alcohol in their systems. As one of them said, "A crime of trickery requires such skill that a man can't afford to drink on the job." A Senate subcommittee found that liquor was allied with organized crime, prostitution, and extortion in corrupting the governments of our states and nation.

In certain very important areas of human life the Christain faith and the drinking of alcohol are in direct competition. This is pointed out by Paul: ". . . do not get drunk with wine, . . . but be filled with the spirit . . ." (EPHESIANS 5:18).

The church competes by satisfying the basic spiritual needs of people:

The church says, "When in trouble, turn to the Lord."

Alcohol says, "When in trouble, turn to drink."

The church says, "When you are frustrated, seek hope from God."

Alcohol says, "When you are frustrated, seek hope from the bottle."

The church says, "When you feel ill at ease in groups, try being yourself and being kind."

Alcohol says, "When you feel ill at ease in groups, forget yourself in drink."

The church says, "When you feel unequal to a task, trust in the Lord and work hard."

Alcohol says, "When you feel unequal to the task, take a drink and plunge ahead."

The gospel meets the problem with a confidence that is based upon fact, an experience based upon the true nature of reality, and a drive that comes from love and not lust. Alcohol meets life's trying experiences with a substance that deadens feelings, destroys true self-confidence, and defeats maturity.

In the personal life drinking becomes a substitute for the gospel. In the moral life drinking becomes an opponent of restraint and virtue. In the physical life drinking becomes not only a killer of the body through homicide and the automobile, but the greatest enemy of sanity. In the political life drinking becomes the ally of forces that seek to destroy the character of government and the moral integrity of foreign policy. The church has good reason for its opposition to drinking!

What then is the message of the church regarding social drinking? First, the church issues a warning against drinking. It does not always say that drinking is an absolute sin, but it affirms that it is a very dangerous practice. As Dinah Shore said, "If a star wishes to reach the heights she should hitch herself to the water wagon."

This warning is based not only on what drinking can do to you but on what it can do to others through you. A drunk never entices another person to drink—alcoholics are repulsive—but young and old are enticed by the "men of distinction" who drink and get by with it. It is not the drunks who are responsible for the increased drinking in society; this blame falls into the lap of the "social" set. It is never Skid Row but the plush cocktail bar that puts pressure on nondrinkers.

Second, the church proclaims its message of moral responsibility. God will hold you responsible for the property, the lives, and the morals which come under the influences you exert. Drinking will not serve as an excuse before the throne of God when you have to answer for the body you broke in an accident, the soul you destroyed in an evening's entertainment, or the children you neglected.

I have worked a great deal with alcoholics during my ministry. So often they tell me that they have done nothing wrong, that they have hurt no one but themselves. But I must remind them that God has created us to be something worthwhile; to be anything less than God has made us to be is a sin.

Third, the church affirms to the world the power of the gospel of Christ. Not long ago I was talking to a preacher who had been an alcoholic and had returned to sanity. When I asked him what the church could do about this growing alcoholic problem, his answer was that we should warn people against the first drink, and should tell them that there is nothing that drink can do for them that the gospel cannot do more effectively.

Where alcohol will ultimately tear down maturity, peace, and sociability, the Christian gospel offers Christ who can give the maturity sought by young people, the independence desired by all free men, the social adapt-

61

ability longed for by the "wallflower," the inner peace that enables one to meet new experiences, and the escape *into* reality rather than escape *from* reality.

If drinking is an answer to a problem in your life, then I suggest that a far more effective answer to that problem—one that will not increase your sense of inferiority, or destroy your ability, or bankrupt you financially, spiritually, or morally—is to be found in the Christian faith. The church offers to drinker and nondrinker alike the gospel of Christ which is the power of God to meet any and all of the problems of life. As the Scriptures say, ". . . be not drunk with wine, but be filled with the Spirit. . . ."

6

a message to men

AN ARTICLE in *Fortune* magazine made this indictment: "If American businessmen are right in the way that
most of them now live, then all of the wise men of the
ages, all the prophets and the saints, were fools. If the
saints were not fools, the businessmen must be."

Certainly this applies not only to many businessmen of
our day but to many political leaders as well. And yet
only a fanatic few would say that these men are all bad.
They love their children and seek to provide what is
best for them; they serve their communities; they are
officials of churches and school boards; they teach in our
Sunday schools and participate in evangelism programs.
These men give great amounts of money for the operation
of welfare agencies, colleges and universities, churches
and youth camps.

The article about these men goes on to say: "The most
casual observer is aware of the transgressions that go on
daily in the American business community. He hears of
tax returns that are outright perjury; he hears of pur-
chasing agents who are taking bribes from suppliers, of
businessmen offering bribes for false testimony, of police
protection of some dubious enterprise. He reads of in-

dustries attempting to suborn state legislators for favorable legislation; he reads of businessmen bestowing favors on government officials to win special privileges. We hear of . . . management acting in collusion with racketeers, of men using prostitution to promote sales of their goods. We hear of businessmen violating the most elementary requirements of city building codes and profiting from rat-infested tenements. We hear of financiers deliberately lying about their operations and the financial condition of their companies to mislead investors so that insiders can make a killing in stock."

Certainly when one adds to this the scandals connected with highway paving, hiring and firing in government offices, censorship, misleading campaign promises, accusations dominated by half-truths and open lies, we have a foundation for applying the accusation to politicians also.

What has happened is that some businessmen and politicians have separated their lives into segments: their worship on Sunday has nothing to do with their political or business world on Monday. Sunday sermons are appropriate if they deal with the problems of youth, juvenile delinquency, and old age, or ways to give comfort to the distressed, to solve the alcohol problem—any area that relates theology to life is appropriate, except business and politics.

There are valid reasons for these split personalities of many business and political leaders. We must first acknowledge that part of the blame falls on many who are recognized as prophets and seers. In their idealism these men sometimes forget that they are living in a realistic world, a world made up of saints and sinners.

They have ceased to strive for improvement because they are willing to accept nothing short of perfection as the first step.

For example, obedience to God makes divorce unnecessary; but Moses had to reckon with the fact that all men are not interested in God. He therefore gave laws regarding divorce. Jesus dealt with this when He said, "For your hardness of heart Moses allowed you to divorce your wives, but from the beginning it was not so" (MATTHEW 19:8). Moses was right to set up rules governing divorce because they protected women and society. The fanatic refuses to recognize this hardness of heart on the part of people and refuses to make social provisions for divorce. The true idealist will recognize that divorce is wrong, but lest a greater wrong be committed he will set up rules for protection of women and children.

Similarly, many people who favor temperance have become fanatics. In their "refusal to compromise with evil" they have ignored the sin in man. They have voted for prohibitionists, completely oblivious to their views on other issues such as foreign relations. They have refused to have any part in seeking to work out the least offensive method for selling alcohol because they will not have any dealings with anything short of complete prohibition. The refusal to take one step toward a goal has made business and political leaders feel that idealism and business have no common meeting place.

Another reason for rejecting idealism has been the complexity of many of our problems. It is not always easy to figure out what is just and honorable in some situations. A just wage does not mean as little wages as one can afford; on the other hand, it does not mean such high wages that a product is priced out of the market.

The complexity of our problems fosters inactivity and submission to pressure. Rather than honestly seeking out the solution most in keeping with our Sunday morning professions of faith, we do nothing. When one adds to this picture the natural tendency toward selfishness and greed, and the fact that we are living in a world where business and politics wink at the practical application of religious faith, one can see why a businessman or a politician who loves his children, supports his church, works for the "Y" and the Scouts, and serves in his civic club, can be accused in such terms as, "If American businessmen are right in the way that most of them now live, then all of the wise men of the ages, all the prophets and the saints were fools. If the saints were not fools, the businessmen must be."

To these men we can apply the great moral themes of the Bible. Read the words of Amos who speaks for God: "I hate, I despise your feasts, and I take no delight in your solemn assemblies. Even though you offer me your burnt offerings and cereal offerings, I will not accept them, and the peace offerings of your fatted beasts I will not look upon. Take away from me the noise of your songs; to the melody of your harps I will not listen. But let justice roll down like waters, and righteousness like an everflowing stream" (5:21-24).

Or read the words of Isaiah: "Bring no more vain offerings; incense is an abomination to me. New moon and sabbath and the calling of assemblies—I cannot endure iniquity and solemn assembly. Your new moons and your appointed feasts my soul hates; they have become a burden to me, I am weary of bearing them. When you spread forth your hands, I will hide my eyes from you; even though you make many prayers, I will not listen; your hands are full of blood" (1:13-15).

Study the words of Micah: "'With what shall I come before the Lord, and bow myself before God on high? Shall I come before him with burnt offerings, with calves a year old? Will the Lord be pleased with thousands of rams, with ten thousands of rivers of oil? Shall I give my first-born for my transgression, the fruit of my body for the sin of my soul?' He has showed you, O man, what is good; and what does the Lord require of you but to do justice, and to love kindness, and to walk humbly with your God?" (6:6-8).

In a land where cattle and oil were wealth, the Israelite temple was becoming rich. People were bringing into the coffers their thousands of rams, their calves, and what seemed like ten thousands of rivers of oil. Businessmen were paying their tithes to make the temple prosperous. They were going beyond the tithe; they were showing their devotion by offering their firstborn children as sacrifices to God. Archaeologists are finding that the origin of the cornerstone was in Palestine, where parents killed a firstborn child, put its body in an urn, and placed the urn in the foundation of a house as a symbol of their devotion to their God.

In the face of such devotion, Micah asked himself, "With what shall I come before the Lord?" and the answer came: ". . . what does the Lord require of you but to do justice, and to love kindness, and to walk humbly with your God?"

The first requirement of God is to do justice. Notice

that this Biblical passage does not say, "to *think* justice." Many of us would substitute thinking justice and talking justice for doing justice.

Justice involves "that to which a man has a right." It is unjust for a teacher to give a boy a grade of D when he deserves an A. It is unjust to give a horse the victor's wreath when he comes in second, unless of course the first horse has committed a foul. Justice involves that to which we—or others—are entitled. John Locke went so far as to say that there can be no justice except where there is private property, but certainly this is not the conception of justice held by the Scriptures. Justice involves our right to property, our right to reputation, our right to marry, to think, to work, to believe.

Any Christian concept of justice must recognize two fundamental premises: the equality and the inequality of men. The doctrine of the equality of men is based upon the story of creation where we are told that God created man in His own image. The doctrine is brought to fulfillment in the words of Jesus: " 'Truly, I say to you, as you did it to one of the least of these my brethren, you did it to me' " (MATTHEW 25:40). Here we have the foundation for justice as written into our Declaration of Independence, which says that man has certain "inalienable rights," and among these are life, liberty, and the pursuit of happiness.

Also true is the Scriptural doctrine of the inequality of men, for we read, "So God created man in his own image, in the image of God he created him; male and female he created them" (GENESIS 1:27). This is the first statement of inequality, an inequality based upon nature and function.

All people have certain rights because they are made in the image of God, but the rights of a child and the rights of a man are not the same. The child has a right to his childhood which involves the right to play and grow, while the man has a right to work. The child should not be overburdened with the responsibilities of working, of voting, or of fighting for his country; nor should the adult have the right to play all day.

The truths of man's equality and inequality are fundamental to man's morals. The equality of rights demands that each individual have and be entitled to keep that which is his. This is vividly illustrated in the case of the Israelite king, Ahab. He saw a piece of property that he wanted, and he offered the owner, Naboth, a fabulous price for it. Because it was a family treasure with sentimental value, Naboth refused to sell. Ahab's wife, not being accustomed to the Israelite conception of justice, arranged for Naboth to be killed and gave the property to the king. Ahab and his wife were denounced by God's prophet because Naboth had a right to his own property and the king had no right to it.

The same thing happened in the case of David and Bathsheba. David wanted Bathsheba, but she was the wife of Uriah. David had Uriah placed in such a position in battle that he was killed, but God's prophet reminded David forcibly that he had no right to Uriah's wife. To take away that to which someone else is entitled is a violation of the fundamental of justice.

Should we come before the Lord with money, or participation in worthwhile organizations? What does the Lord require of us but to do justice? It came as a brilliant revelation to me when I realized that this passage said we must do justice and must love mercy. It is most significant that it does not say we must love justice and do mercy. To wish to do justice or to love to do it is not enough. Mercy, on the other hand, means giving to the individual more than that to which he is entitled. God, through punishment, gives to the individual that to which he is entitled; in mercy He gives forgiveness and salvation.

Justice requires a bank to give to each despositor all he has deposited, plus the interest that has been promised. Justice does not require payment of a cent more. The banker may know that the money deposited by a retired man in 1935 is not yielding the returns necessary to keep him in food today. In mercy, therefore, he may send a contribution every month, or he may help him to get a part-time job that will not be too strenuous. The banker has no right to take money from other depositors to give in charity.

Justice must be the guiding fundamental of all business and government activity. Business and political leaders, men, women and children—all are enjoined to do justice, to love mercy, and to walk humbly with their God.

The final imperative is to walk with God. There is a qualifying word: walk *humbly* with your God. I shall never forget a businessman who said, "I don't care what the Bible says—this is the way I am going to run my business!" That man claimed to walk with God, but he did not walk humbly. Walking humbly with God involves the attitude of learning from God. A business magazine made an interesting suggestion to businessmen. It proposed that business enterprises set up studies of business ethics. This would involve, at the governmental level, the appointment of chaplains who would do far more than open the sessions of legislature with a prayer. It would involve the appointment of men who would study legislation from the ethical point of view and seek to give ethical leadership to legislative bodies.

In business it would mean that large corporations would have someone at the vice-presidential level who would study policy, management-labor problems, advertising, and even production, from the standpoints of justice and equity rather than merely legality. The firm that can afford legal counsel can certainly afford moral counsel to bring it in line with the truth of God. Under this plan small-business men would meet together and invite for discussion those who understood both the problems of their businesses and the implications of Christian ethics.

We have many chaplains in our day, and many organizations of Christian businessmen, but all too often they are concerned with prayers, with the bringing of rams and rivers of oil to the Kingdom, and with the offering of their sons for sacrifice. If we are to be pleasing to God, we must walk humbly with Him and seek to find His will for our lives rather than contenting ourselves with the cattle and the oil that we bring to the church.

The magazine indictment is true. Either our businessmen and politicians are wise and the saints were fools, or the businessmen and politicians are fools and Micah and Jesus were wise. We do not question who is right. Acknowledging that Micah, Amos, and Jesus are right, we must call upon our business and political leaders to *do justice, love mercy, and walk humbly with God.*

7

this is mine

BILLY SUNDAY once said, "When a man starts arguing that stealing is not a sin, don't argue with him—search him."

The owner of a ladies' shoe and handbag shop tells of a woman who used to buy some of his most expensive evening bags. He noticed that she frequently returned them two or three days later. One morning she came in to return a particular bag and when she told him that the bag was unsatisfactory, he replied, "That is such a shame. You seemed to be enjoying it so much last night when this picture was taken." He then showed her a picture which had been taken at a fashionable party the previous evening—she was showing the handbag to one of her friends. If that had been an isolated instance of dishonesty it would not be a serious matter, but our retail sales concerns say that dishonesty is not an isolated instance.

The head shipping-clerk of a Chicago department store was to be honored for twenty-five years of faithful service. Three days before the quarter-century pin was to be awarded he was caught stealing a $250 evening dress from the store. His explanation: "I wanted something nice for my wife to wear to the award dinner."

In a recent year bank robbers in the United States stole $1,300,000. During the same time the employees of banks walked out with $9,500,000. The Federal Bureau of Investigation calculates that all the nation's burglars, pickpockets, armed robbers, and auto thieves steal less than the embezzlers.

Evidence such as the above has convinced me that it is very much in order to study the Biblical concept of property. Some of the Biblical laws are utterly impractical for a modern industrial civilization, but they illustrate some fundamental principles of ethical living.

One of the most interesting sections of Hebrew law deals with the year of Jubilee. Fundamental to the concept of Jubilee was a law that no property could be sold in perpetuity. If it was sold it had to be returned to the original owners at the year of Jubilee. To seek to sell property for all time was a sin. The law says, "The land shall not be sold in perpetuity, for the land is mine . . ." (LEVITICUS 25:23).

Jubilee came every fifty years. If we still lived under this law we would be able to give leases only until the year 2000. In 1951 we could have given a forty-nine year lease, but in the year 1990 we would only be able to give a ten-year lease. At the year 2000 all property would be returned to the original owners.

Now there were two practical reasons for this law. First of all, it kept one individual or family from amassing all the land of Israel and making the other families virtual slaves. The land belonged to the families and it could not even be sold in perpetuity to the king.

This law also prevented a man from destroying economic or social opportunities for his children and grandchildren. The man who had no property in Israel had as much chance for economic or social progress as the man of today who does not have an education. In that day property was to opportunity what education is to opportunity today. It did not guarantee success, but without it success was less likely to be achieved. A man's right to sell his property was therefore limited by his responsibility to the common good and to future generations.

Another series of interesting laws were those concerning oxen that gored and wells that were left unprotected. According to Biblical law, if a man owned an ox and it gored another ox to death, the offending ox would have been sold and its price divided between its owner and the man whose ox had been killed. The carcass of the dead ox was also to be divided. If the ox had ever gored before and had not been kept away from the neighbor's ox, then the owner of the ox that did the goring was required to give his ox in place of the one that had been killed.

If this law were transferred to modern society and you had an automobile accident in which you destroyed another person's car, you would have to sell your car and give half of the proceeds to the owner of the other car. You would also have to divide the sale price of his car. If this were your second negligent accident, you would have to give your car to the other man and the destroyed car would become yours.

Similar Old Testament laws say that if a man started a fire and it got out of hand and burned another man's field or house, he had to pay for the field or house. We are responsible not only for preserving our property for

74

the common good and for future generations, but also for damage done by our property. Man has a social obligation that is implied in his ownership of property.

One of the fascinating laws of the Old Testament dealt with the forgotten sheaf of wheat. If in the midst of harvesting the wheat crop a man forgot a sheaf of wheat in the field, the law did not allow him to go back, pick it up, and put it with the rest of his wheat. He had to leave it in the field for the orphans, the widows, and the sojourners.

This law is illustrated in the Book of Ruth. When Boaz found that Ruth was gleaning close to his fields, he ordered his men to drop some of the wheat they were gathering. If Ruth saw the sheaves of wheat, she as a widow was perfectly within her rights to pick them up and take them as her own. Similarly the harvesters were not allowed to harvest the corners of the fields.

While a man technically owned land, by law he was not allowed to forget the poor, the orphans, and the widows. Thus a man's property rights were limited by the needs of the poor around him.

One of the most severe denunciations of Israel is found in the Book of Malachi. The prophet, speaking for God, says to the people, "Will man rob God?" The people immediately respond in amazement, "How are we robbing thee?" And the reply comes back, "In your tithes and offerings" (3:8). The laws of the tithes were very numerous and inclusive in Israel. The people were to give the first fruits of their crops to God, and ten per cent of all the rest. This was God's royalty on the property and the talents He had given to man. Failing to pay the tithe was the same as failing to pay one's rent.

Frequently circumstances force me to rent a car and I usually keep it one or two days. I have never been able to satisfy the car rental agency by returning the car without paying them rent and mileage on it. They usually want the car returned, plus a fee for each day, and in addition a certain amount of money per mile. God deals with man in exactly the same way. It is not enough to give ourselves and our talents back to Him after we have finished using them. There is the matter of royalty that we must pay to Him. This royalty is figured at ten per cent of our incomes. Refusing to pay is the equivalent of robbing God.

We should note one more restriction on our property rights. It is best expressed by Jesus in the parable of the talents. You will recall that He told the story of a businessman who was going on a long journey. He entrusted certain of his assets to three of his servants and when he returned each of them was expected to repay the original talents, plus the interest which he had earned with them. The first two men doubled the original sums. The third man had not invested the money and returned only what had been given to him. In disgust the owner took the money away from him and gave it to one of the men who had invested wisely.

What we have been given is to be used to produce more. If we do not use what God has given us, He will take it away from us and give it to someone else. We have here a basic premise of property rights: use or lose. It was on the basis of this premise that our forefathers took land away from the Indians who were not using the American continent in any productive way. Our forefathers therefore took it from them, giving them a mere pittance for it.

From our brief survey of Scripture we have found that no man has absolute property rights. God keeps the final and ultimate ownership of all property and turns it over to us to hold and use for Him. But our trusteeship has certain definite restrictions imposed on it by God. No man has a right to say, "This property is mine. I will do with it what I please." He can do what he pleases with his land, home, automobile, brains, body, stocks, and money—only as long as what he pleases is in keeping with the general rules and regulations given by God.

Having examined these Old Testament principles of property rights, let us look at present-day problems. One of the most serious problems society faces today is the rising tide of embezzlement. The tragedy in current embezzlement is that it is carried out by people who are not considered to be in the category of thieves. Consider the description of the average embezzler as given in *Fortune* magazine:

He is in his thirties, is married, has one or two children. He lives in a respectable neighborhood, drives a medium-priced car, and once in a while travels on the weekend. Whatever his secret life, he usually looks like a good mixer and is active in the community; often as not, he's a church officer. Usually he has had a couple of job promotions, partly because he has been around the firm for a while, and partly because he has slightly better than average ability, works hard, and seems willing to accept responsibility. In one study of 1001 cases, 270 of the embezzlers held supervisory or executive positions . . . lawyers are in a singularly tempting position as trustees and estate executors . . . when a man's busi-

77

ness is in trouble embezzlement often seems to be the only way out.

If we try to face this problem of embezzlement we will find two areas of responsibility that come within the scope of the church. The church brings a message of redemption and our society is full of guilty men. As Christians it is not our responsibility to bring the guilty to justice but it is our responsibility to bring the guilty to redemption. Jesus Christ died for the ungodly; all of us stand as sinners, needing the grace of God. Through our own forgiveness of those who have sinned, we must bring them to know the complete acceptance and forgiveness of God.

There is despair in the embezzler. One man put it this way: "One day I realized I was in too deep. It was like awakening from a dream. All of a sudden it hit me. I wasn't going to pay it back. How could I? I was a thief." These people know that they have cut themselves off from community, friends, and family. They panic: some run; some try sleeping pills; others choose a gun; still others use the automobile. But there is hope for them. Jesus Christ can make them pure, can restore them as He has restored millions of others before them.

We in the church are also in the business of preventing sin. It is our aim to set such a high ideal in the minds of our membership, to so surround them with upright people, to teach the power and meaning of prayer, that embezzlement will be made impossible.

One article on embezzlement says that it usually is accompanied by one of the three "B's": booze, bookies, and babes. By offering the means to keep people from the three B's—friendly support and the power to withstand temptation—the church can prevent many embezzlements from ever taking place.

Let us turn to another problem, that of debt payment. One of our financial journals reports that two of the three companies putting out universal credit cards are in serious financial trouble because people do not pay their debts. In talking with newsboys one can learn of the difficulty they have collecting from some people in financially elite neighborhoods. Department stores report that in many cities some of the leading citizens do not pay their bills.

In the Old Testament there is an interesting law dealing with the payment of servants: "You shall not oppress a hired servant who is poor and needy, . . . you shall give him his hire on the day he earns it, before the sun goes down . . . lest he cry against you to the Lord, and it be sin in you" (DEUTERONOMY 24:14-15).

In speaking of those who refuse to pay just debts, the Bible says, ". . . all who do such things [refuse to pay obligations], all who act dishonestly, are an abomination to the Lord . . ." (DEUTERONOMY 25:16). Again the church has a concern here.

So much of our upaid obligations come from overpurchasing—we buy without thinking. One of the tasks of the church is to teach such a high moral standard that people will not purchase more than they can afford.

To find out whether you are overpurchasing, ask how many times you have had to reorganize or refinance your obligations in the past five years. To get into a financial bind once is understandable, but to stay in one means moral irresponsibility.

A friend of mine retired during the 1920's. He and his wife had good health and lived until they were almost one hundred years old. When they had retired they owned their own home and had money invested to give them what they thought would be an adequate income for the rest of their lives. The money that would have paid for food, clothes, and medical bills in the twenties paid for less and less throughout the forties and fifties. Finally the couple had to sell their home and live on charity. Inflation had made almost worthless their life savings. Inflation can be a thief.

Part of this inflation comes from our governmental finance policies: for the sake of more roads we build a debt for the future; for the sake of buildings and salaries for teachers we increase our future obligations. Surely society must provide education for its children. Should we not be honest enough to pay taxes for what we get instead of adding to our debt? Should we not be responsible enough to pay off past obligations instead of increasing them? It is not a matter of the rightness or wrongness of the projects for which we spend money. It is a matter of our irresponsibility which causes us to demand services from our government when we are not willing to pay for them.

In our study of property rights we mentioned the Old Testament law of responsibility for damages done by a man's ox or an open well. Our society has many open wells of which this commandment could speak.

A few years ago a man told me that I should invest some money in houses that were poorly constructed, had outdoor toilets, no electricity, and no underpinning. I was told that I could get my money back in four years.

80

When I asked him how I could get such high returns on
the houses he pointed out that there was no other place
for the Negroes to live. I asked why they did not build
their own houses rather than pay exorbitant rents. His
reply was classic: "We have them where we want them.
Who would sell them property?" What bank would lend
them money at six per cent when the bank directors, by
renting homes, could get a return of twenty-five per cent?

Well, an epidemic hit the families in those houses, and
poor sanitation was blamed. A number of people died.
But it is also interesting to note that the epidemic spread
to the home of one of the bank directors and his child
was among those who died.

A man who keeps a piece of property that is dangerous
to the life and health of people is violating a fundamental
of the moral law of property rights. These are not absolute
rights, but limited rights; they are limited by our responsibilities to our neighbors and to society.

God has made laws of property. By refusing to pay our
rent, our royalty of ten per cent, we have been robbing
God and have kept the church from moving forward. We
have crippled ourselves.

We have gotten away from calling things by their real
names. We feel that "stealing" is a dirty word, but
taking equipment from the concern where we work,
collecting towels or silver from hotels, refusing to pay our
tithes to God, developing programs of inflation, encum-
bering future generations—these are personal matters with
which morality is not supposed to deal. To such a world,
the Word of God speaks His command: "Thou shalt not
steal."

8

the bible speaks
to our racial problem

A STRIFE-TORN church sets a poor example for a divided world. Today the most serious manifestation of strife within the church can be seen in our racial separation.

Those of us in the South receive small comfort from the realization that ours is not the only part of the world facing racial difficulties. New York, California, Mexico, India—all parts of the world—are troubled over similar problems. The universality of a problem, however, is no excuse for ignoring its reality. Many cities have a problem of water shortage, but some cities have done something about it.

Finding a solution is made difficult because the issue is complicated by the battle between the laws of the central government and the rights of individual states. It is further complicated by vote-seeking politicians and irresponsible agitators who are not sincerely interested in solutions.

Our love for the church and for our institutions is sometimes a deterrent to action. We cannot be satisfied with any solution that splits a church or renders our educational system ineffective.

Guilt and defensiveness play their parts in our thinking. We all know that slavery is indefensible and that while our schools were separate they were never equal until our fear of court action gave us new incentive. We are deeply conscious of the violation of Negro womanhood by white men, a violation which has left so few pure Negroes among us. We are also defensive about the knowledge that a Negro has little chance of getting any job above the level of the "bucket brigade" in city or in business.

In solving our problem we have a great asset that is not present in other parts of the world: there is a background of love between individual whites and Negroes that has dated back for two centuries. Many of us remember that one of the first hands to guide our toddling steps was a black one. There was many a "Mammy" who spent part of every afternoon preparing cookies for "her boys" when they came home from school.

Henry Grady, speaking in Dallas at the turn of the century, said:

"I want no truer soul than that which moved the trusty slave, who, for years, while my father fought with armies that barred his freedom, slept every night at my mother's door, holding her and her children as safe as if her husband stood guard, and ready to lay down his humble life on her threshold. . . .

"I rejoice that when freedom came to him after years of waiting, it was all the sweeter because the black hands from which the shackles fell were stainless of a single crime against the helpless ones confided to his care."

We are also aware that we are fighting a worldwide battle against other faiths, the most militant of which is communism. No longer can the Communists point to breadlines, sweat shops, child labor, or depressions. Rather, they defame us by sending American Negroes such as Paul Robeson on speaking tours of Africa to expose the worst part of our racial situation. Islam uses this weakness also; it is to our shame that in parts of Africa Mohammedanism is gaining ten converts for each convert won to the Christian faith. What is happening in Africa is happening in other parts of the world.

Our worldwide evangelism is suffering because of our racial situation. Our faith is being ridiculed because of our sins and failure. Our own conscience is being seared over some facets of the problem. We are troubled and seek a way out. Those who advocate patience must recognize that patience runs thin after a hundred years of waiting.

In our distress we cry out, "Is there a word from God?" The cry comes back, "Christ is the answer." I am convinced that Christ is the answer. Perhaps the trouble is that we are as much afraid of this answer as we are of the diagnosis of our earthly physicians. But in the Great Physician there is power for the healing of the nations. Let us turn to Him in our dilemma. We know that the "light of the world" can shed light on our difficulties.

The first word that comes back to us is God's statement that He ". . . made from one every nation of men to live on all the face of the earth . . ." (ACTS 17:26). As Louis Evans put it, "There is no doctrine of the Fatherhood of God without the brotherhood of man." We affirm this Fatherhood of God every time we pray, "Our Father who art in heaven. . . ."

84

There are those who will read the statement from Acts and will say that the next part of the quotation says that God has set the bounds of the nations' habitation. One of my friends says that this proves that the Negro should stay in Africa. Such reasoning, if taken to its logical conclusion, would mean that the white man should leave the United States also and go back to Europe, turning the United States back to the Indians.

Some people say that God intended some men to be slaves; they quote the curse that ordered Canaan to be the servant of his brothers. But these people do not read the story thoroughly. The curse was not pronounced by God but by Noah—and while Noah was suffering from a hangover. It should also be noted that some of the descendants of Canaan were the Assyrians and the Phoenicians.

When we pray the Lord's Prayer we are affirming the brotherhood under the Fatherhood of God. How I wish that white and Negro leaders could get together and discuss their mutual problems only after praying the Lord's Prayer. This should be easy in a sanctuary that Jesus called a "house of prayer for all the nations" (MARK 11:17).

When the church in Galatia was about to separate into racial or ethnic groups, Paul wrote these words: ". . . in Christ Jesus you are all sons of God, through faith. . . . There is neither Jew nor Greek, there is neither slave nor free, there is neither male nor female; for you are all one in Christ Jesus" (GALATIANS 3:26-28). That is why we can sing with John Oxenham:

> In Christ there is no East or West,
> In Him no South or North,

But one great Fellowship of Love
Throughout the whole wide earth.

Join hands then, Brothers of the Faith,
Whate'er your race may be!—
Who serves my Father as a son
Is surely kin to me.

Our Lord said, " '. . . as you did it to one of the least of these my brethren, you did it to me'" (MATTHEW 25:40). Couple this with His statement: " '. . . he who rejects you rejects me . . .'" (LUKE 10:16). Perhaps many of our churches are weak because we have rejected Jesus at the door when He came as a hungry beggar, a poorly clothed woman, or a Negro. Having rejected Him at the door, how can we expect to find Him inside?

Knowing that Christ may be dwelling in any man who walks up to the door of any church, and knowing that He may be present in anyone who sits beside us, can we reject Him? The rich young ruler made the mistake of rejecting Him because of money. May this not happen to anyone because of race.

We cannot escape the realization that we are united as Christian brothers through our love for one another. It is interesting to note that Christ gave one great commandment to guide our relationships with each other: "Thou shalt love thy neighbor as thyself" (MATTHEW 19:19, KJV). He also described one test by which all the world would judge the truth of our discipleship: "By this all men will know that you are my disciples, if you have love for one another" (JOHN 13:35).

George Washington Carver, one of the great Negroes of

American history, was asked by a group of ministers what they could do to improve race relations. His answer was simple and frank: "Your actions speak so loud I cannot hear what you are saying. You have too much religion and not enough Christianity—too many creeds and not enough performance."

The world sees through the sham of our pretensions. We all know the temptation to water down the word "love" to include our resentments and our arrogance.

Do Europeans look at the South and say, "Behold how these southern white men love the southern Negro"? We must be honest with ourselves. The great commandment and the great test of discipleship are involved in our brotherhood. Where do you stand with regard to this commandment and this test?

We must also understand that we are united as brothers by our fear of the wrath of God. Jesus says, "Whoever causes one of these little ones who believe in me to sin [or to stumble], it would be better for him if a great millstone were hung round his neck and he were thrown into the sea" (MARK 9:42). When I remember this verse and see thousands of Africans turning to communism, to Islam, or to humanism because of the racial attitude in the southern white church, I am petrified with fear.

In Deuteronomy and in Acts we are told that God is no respecter of persons. Later on in James we read, "My brethren, show no partiality as you hold the faith of our Lord Jesus Christ, the Lord of glory. . . . if you show partiality, you commit sin, and are convicted by the law as transgressors" (2:1, 9). James is saying that to have respect of the persons who are seated in the church is a sin.

87

When I hear that someone has walked out of a sanctuary or changed churches because of the presence of a Negro, my heart trembles for him. Such a person is living in sin. We are warned, ". . . flee from the wrath to come" (MATTHEW 3:7).

Christians are united as brothers by their eternal destiny. Heaven may be as exclusive as a country club, but not in terms of what we call "the right people." Those who wish to find the "right people" are going to find it difficult to fulfill their desire for eternity. Many of the right people and many from the wrong side of the track will be in hell —and many of them will be in heaven.

Those who cannot be happy associating with people of another race on an equal basis on this earth may find heaven very disagreeable. John says, ". . . I looked, and behold, a great multitude which no man could number, from every nation, from all tribes and peoples and tongues, standing before the throne . . ." (REVELATION 7:9-10). The church is supposed to reflect the Kingdom of God; we pray, "thy kingdom come." Are you willing for your church to reflect heaven in its racial attitudes?

We Christians are united by our aim in society. The Kingdom we seek is one of justice, brotherhood, opportunity, and honor. If we mean what we pray, we cannot work for something that is unjust, unbrotherly, or for something which deprives a man of his opportunities or his rights.

Finally, we are united by our dedication to the principle of the second mile. Perhaps we should call it the principle of sticking one's neck out. It affirms that we will not only refuse to participate in evil but that we will go the second mile to eradicate evil. We will reach out a hand to help those who are oppressed.

It would be fine if we could build a house by the side of the road and watch the rest of the world go by, but we have been called to be "the light of the world," "the salt of the earth"; we are to heal the earth's wounds, to relieve the oppressed, to remedy injustices, to solve man's problems. Our dedication to the principle of the second mile puts us in direct conflict with the evil about us and should make us aggressive in our stand for Christ and His Kingdom.

Much more could be said but surely enough has been said to help all Christians to understand why in 1865 the General Assembly of the Presbyterian Church in the United States, meeting in Macon, Georgia, with Dr. George Howe of Charleston, South Carolina, as moderator, took the following action:

WHEREAS, the colored people never stood in any other relation to the church than that of human beings lost with us in the fall of Adam, and redeemed with us by the infinitely meritorious death and sacrifice of Christ, and participants with us in all the benefits and blessings of the gospel; and

WHEREAS, our churches, pastors and people have always recognized this claim to Christian equality and brotherhood, and have rejoiced to have them associated in the Christian union and communion in the public services of the sanctuary;

RESOLVED, 1st, that the abolition of slavery by the civil and military powers, has not altered the relations as above defined, in which our church stands to the colored people, nor in any way lessened the debt of love and service which we

89

> owe to them, nor interest with which we should
> still desire to be associated with them in all the
> privileges of our common Christianity. . . ."

This conviction has been reiterated time and time again
in many churches in the South.

If we believe that Christ is the answer, and, if we believe that the Bible reflects the mind of Christ, then we
must accept these Biblical principles and the truth that
the church has proclaimed through the centuries. These
principles must guide our actions in the matter of race.

We must be willing to take our faith into our lives.
We must be willing to affirm that Christ is the answer
to our mounting racial problem. We must be willing to
follow Him.

We have now come to the point where we must ask
how we can relate these great doctrines of our faith to
our racial problem. One of our national magazines pub-
lished an article about race by Billy Graham, in which
he made several helpful suggestions that can serve as a
guide for our thinking. Part of his suggestion deals with
our inner life. We must constantly reaffirm that when a
person is converted—truly won to the Lord Jesus Christ—
the Holy Spirit comes into his life and drives out antagonisms, hatreds, dishonesty, and expediency.

Dr. Graham reminds us that Christ touches our emotions, casts out hatred, malice, and arrogance, and fills
our hearts with love. He touches our minds, casts out dishonesty, and gives us a sincere desire to see and know
the truth. He touches our wills, casts out expediency, and
makes us willing to take up a cross for that which we
believe.

The best place to start to do something about the race problem is in our own families. We are surprised at some of the things our children bring home from school and playground. They hear Negroes called "niggers" and this sounds cute to them. They do not know that Negroes despise that word and that using it is like slapping them in the face. We can teach our children that they are not to disparage other races, that they are not to be offensive to a man because his skin is not the same color as theirs. We can acquaint our children with some national and church heroes who were of other races. If we do not know of any, perhaps it is because we have not sought to acquaint ourselves with them. Our families might grow together spiritually if we could spend time getting to know great Christians and great leaders of other races.

In the play *South Pacific* one of the songs says, "You've got to be taught to hate." There is so much hatred and antagonism in our world that no longer do people need to be taught to hate. Today we must teach people to love. Perhaps this is our most important area of service as we seek to meet the rising tide of racism.

Billy Graham also suggests that we must accept our responsibilities in the business world. Every time a Negro has to rely on a union or court action to help him get a job he is tempted to resent the white man who has to be forced to give him a job. He knows he is not wanted and he begins to hate. The white man who is forced to employ a Negro resents the force put upon him. And so hatred mushrooms. As individuals we can take the initiative and prove to be the friend of the person best qualified for a job, irrespective of race.

We can take a stand for love and brotherhood in

our churches. Many voices are being raised in the churches to protest the Christian stand on race. Where are the people who will put pressure on the church to be Christian? Where are the people who expect the church to follow the Bible? Have you told your officers that if anyone cuts his pledge because the church is Christian that you will help to make up the deficit?

The time has come for the church to recognize that in Christ there is the answer to this and every other problem of life. And it is time for the church to dedicate herself to following the answer that Christ has given to us.

This is God's battle and when any Christian is ostracized over this matter, we can only regret that God has been excluded also. There are times when ministers feel very lonely, but when we look up to God we know that we are not alone.

We can be Christian in our daily contacts. An ugly word spoken on a bus, a disparaging word uttered by a clerk, or an arrogant word uttered to a servant can be the beginning of hatred.

While watching the news on television I saw a University of Mississippi student look straight into the camera and say that if James Meredith stayed on that campus he would be killed. I saw the hatred and the evil in that boy's face. As I watched him the thought suddenly crossed my mind, "That boy must have been to church. Has no one taught him about the Fatherhood of God? About being a brother to all Christians through the indwelling Christ? About the wrath of God and the nature of eternity? Has no one taught him about love?" Then I wondered, "Could that boy have grown up in a church where I preached? Could he have come from one of our homes?"

Then I had to pray from the depths of my heart, "God, No! God, No!"

My mind goes back to two ministers in the South who during the 1920's and 1930's sought to teach the truth of God regarding race. These men were maligned and rebuffed. Had the South heeded them and other such Christians there would have been no riot in Albany, Georgia, no bayonets in Little Rock, Arkansas, no deaths in Oxford, Mississippi. Had the South heeded, there would have been no threats of Mohammedanism in Africa or of communism in India. Oh, that we had faced this problem thirty years ago!

I think about my eight-year-old son Charlie, and about all our children. Are we going to hand this problem on to them after the time has run out on the reserve of love and brotherhood? Are we going to add two more decades of disgraceful incidents, hatred, and fear to further complicate any solution?

I look at the cross and see Christ dying for the world. I see Him dying for you and for me and for all men. Will His death and resurrection be in vain because we prefer our sin to His Kingdom? Is the wrath of God going to be the only eternity our people will know?

9

shall I go
to a faith healer?

IN THE Shrine of Guadalupe in Mexico City there is a healing room containing a number of glass-enclosed relics. Thousands of sick people file into that room each week; they place their hands on the affected parts of their bodies, rub the glass enclosing the relics, rub themselves again, and pray. Adjoining the healing room is a room where the walls are covered with little tin models of human bones and organs. When a person feels that he has been healed through his prayer, he buys a tin model and takes it to the cathedral where it is hung on the wall of this room to encourage others to seek health through prayer and faith.

A doctor who was seeking a license to practice medicine in Mexico was asked what he would do if he could do but one thing to improve the poor health situation in Mexico. He replied that he would destroy the Shrine of Guadalupe. Behind this doctor's statement is the fact that when the church emphasizes miraculous healing, it keeps people from going to doctors. The Shrine of Guadalupe does not encourage the use and practice of medicine; it pushes deeper into the minds of the people the conviction

were not cured because of unrepented sin or because of a lack of faith is to twist the New Testament beyond understanding.

Another fact to be remembered is that disease, not pain, is the enemy of mankind. A *Reader's Digest* article entitled "The Why of Aches and Pains" told the story of a twenty-eight-year-old stenographer who lived in western Canada. She had been born without a sense of pain and her body was a "mass of scars and bruises" because she lacked the warning of danger that pain provides. She had often suffered serious burns because the smell of scorched flesh was her first inkling of injury. She had been repeatedly hospitalized for infections of a kind which the rest of us avoid because pain warns us that we are in need of medical care. She also lacked internal responses to pain.

Our body responds to the pain alarm in a number of ways: blood which ordinarily circulates through the skin and the abdominal organs is re-routed to the brain, lungs, and muscles; the heart beats faster and blood pressure rises—all preparatory to taking action against the source of pain.

Faith can obliterate pain—so can hypnosis or aspirin—but removal of the pain usually leaves the disease untouched. Thus the removal of pain is one of the most dangerous practices that doctor, minister, or psychologist can attempt. Overcoming pain without removing the disease is like putting stoppers in your ears because there is a bad knock in the motor of your car. When a doctor relieves pain so that he can treat the patient, that is one thing. When a religious or medical quack relieves pain or its symptoms without treating the disease, that is the height of folly. If disease is our enemy, then pain is one of our greatest friends. Not all the effects of disease and suffering have to be bad. My mind turns back frequently to a book by Betsey Barton. As a teen-ager Miss Barton was injured in an automobile accident which left her a hopeless cripple. In the opening chapter of her book, she says, "There are . . . two tragic facts in human existence: We do not appreciate what we have until we lose it. And we only advance through suffering. . . . Wisdom and vision are granted to few, and the few that gain these do so . . . in the degree that they are sensitive, in the degree that they suffer."

Suffering, disease, and loss seem to be musts in the life of man if he is ever to scale the heights of self-discipline, character, patience, and tenderness that will make him fit for the Kingdom of God. But the results of disease and sickness are not always positive. Man's soul can also be destroyed by sickness: he can grow either more selfish or more concerned for others; he can grow impatient or he can learn patience; he can grow tender or hard. The seed of suffering in our lives can bring forth good or bad fruit, depending on our attitudes toward it.

This does not mean that we should take disease stoically. One of the greatest results of disease should be man's hatred for this enemy. If a villain attacks a loved one, a man would be less than a man if he does not devote much of his energy to seeking to protect the one he loves. God meant for suffering to so inflame us with enmity against the real cause of trouble that we will fight the enemy to the best of our ability for the rest of our lives.

The Christian faith can and does deal with the

100

problem of sickness in many ways. In the first place the church can produce healthy spirits whose bodies are less susceptible to illness. By strengthening their faith in God the church can help people to avoid ulcers. By encouraging forgiving spirits the church can help people to avoid the bodily weaknesses hatred breeds. By nurturing loving trust in God the Christian faith can release people from some of the stresses and strains of life. By molding Christian character the church can remove the causes of syphilis and alcoholism.

The church can also seek to fight disease with all methods at its disposal. Most of our hospitals were built by the Christian church or through the interest of Christian doctors. One of the great factors that has sent many men into the study of medicine is the desire to follow in the footsteps of the Great Physician.

The church must never forget to pray for the sick. Just as we would not refuse to take medicine to a person who needed it, so we must not forget those who need our prayers in the hours of their sickness. Through visiting, through preaching, through our own faith, we must seek to help the sick find new sources of spiritual power, new depths of Christian character, new heights of Christian love. We must do our best to see that months spent in hospitals are not wasted, but are months in which a person can grow more and more Christlike.

We cannot allow our resentment against any form of evil to become an impotent memory. Rather, it must become a vaccination within us which we will spread to all society so that the scourges that have destroyed homes and families, talents and abilities, will be wiped from the face of the earth.

101

When Christ's body, the church, is living in the world, it too will not have to make claims of its divine origin. It will point to the evidence of the sick being healed.

10

and so he left you

WHEN ONE partner in a marriage announces that the marriage is over, the resulting shock to the other partner is extremely severe. The death of a loved one seldom leaves scars as serious as those left by divorce or separation. Both separation and death involve numerous problems of loneliness, financial security, emotional stability, and social relationships.

In addition to the problems caused by death, separation adds other difficulties: a sense of failure in life's most important human relationship; a feeling of resentment toward those involved in the separation; a distrust of other people; and those special times of frustration and embarrassment centering around visiting hours to the children, sharing birthdays, Christmas, graduation, and marriage.

When a person comes to me with this problem, he usually asks why God allowed it to happen to him. The question itself indicates an inadequate understanding of God. God does not send divorce to people; God made people free. But with freedom comes the right to make a mess of marriage and to refuse to act like adults. The suggestion that God gave us separation and divorce is a defamation of the character of God and a refusal to face the real problems of man. If God sent divorce, then man's great need is for protection from a capricious God. Man's need is not for protection from God, but for redemption by God so that he can be free from the evil that leads to divorce.

How should a Christian react when divorce is suggested? Some say, "If you really love him, give him the divorce." Others say, "Give it to him, but make it tough on him." Still others suggest, "Save the marriage for the sake of the children."

Christians must go beyond an examination of one's love for one's mate, or hatred of the evil he has done, or the needs of the children. We must study the nature of marriage itself as expressed by the marriage vows. I have yet to find a marriage vow that says, "I, John, take thee, Sue, to be my wedded wife; and I do promise and covenant before God and these witnesses to be thy loving and faithful husband as long as I feel that I love you, or until I find someone else I love, or until your mother gives us difficulty." Our concept of marriage is that it is ". . . in joy and in sorrow, in sickness and in health, in plenty and in want, for better or worse, as long as we both shall live."

Marriage is the most permanent of all human relationships. When our daughters get married we "give them away," symbolizing that upon maturity the parent-child relationship is dissolved. But there is no provision in God's law for giving away our wives or our husbands. Parenthood is temporary; marriage is permanent.

The Bible sums this up with the statement ". . . that if any brother has a wife who is an unbeliever, and she consents to live with him, he should not divorce her. If any woman has a husband who is an unbeliever, and he consents to live with her, she should not divorce him. . . . But if the unbelieving partner desires to separate, let it be so; in such a case the brother or sister is not bound" (I CORINTHIANS 7:12-13, 15). Accepting this point of view, many Christian lawyers refuse to handle divorce cases.

The fact that your mate has asked for a divorce in no way alters the responsibilities of marriage. You may have to deal with the problem as you would have to deal with your child's problem of running away. Even if the child does run away, that does not change the basic responsibilities of parenthood.

Society has accepted two basic responsibilities of marriage, based upon the Word of God: financial support and the sexual relationship. When the Bible says that the man who does not care for his own household is worse than an infidel, it is speaking of the man who does not support his family financially. No amount of disgust at his wife or dissatisfaction with his home supersedes a husband's responsibility to support the wife he has taken and the children he has sired. An attraction to another person is not a valid excuse for violating this responsibility.

The same applies to the intimate relationships of marriage. Sex is not to be accepted or rejected on the basis of liking or loving someone. If love were the justification for sex, then a husband would be justified in having relations with any woman he thought he loved, and children would be moral in having premarital relations. The Bible says that sexual relations apart from marriage constitute adultery; and it stamps its approval upon all such relationships within marriage, even though the couple have never seen each other until the time of their marriage.

105

"The husband should give to his wife her conjugal rights, and likewise the wife to her husband. . . . Do not refuse one another . . ." (I CORINTHIANS 7:3, 5).

Marriage should be more than the physical matters of financial support and physical relationships. A man and woman have pledged themselves to love each other, and this command to love applies even to our enemies. Did not Jesus say, " 'Love your enemies . . .' " (LUKE 6:27), and " '. . . pray for them which despitefully use you, and persecute you' " (MATTHEW 5:44, KJV)?

The matter of loving our enemies applies in marriage and parenthood as much as in any of life's other relationships. Surely there are times when our children become the enemies of our peace of mind, of our physical well-being, of our spiritual strength. Even though they tell us that they do not love us, that they prefer someone else —even though they violate every moral and spiritual principle we have taught them—we will perform the acts of love toward them. It may seem impossible, but it is often true that the mother loves most the child who has treated her worst. We can love those who misuse us.

Here is one description of love: "Love is patient and kind; love is not jealous or boastful; it is not arrogant or rude. Love does not insist on its own way; it is not irritable or resentful; it does not rejoice at wrong, but rejoices in the right. Love bears all things, believes all things, hopes all things . . ." (I CORINTHIANS 13:4-7).

The spiritual strength to love a wayward husband comes from the same source as the spiritual strength to love a wayward child. Having determined that marriage is permanent, that you will maintain your part of its responsibilities, that you will love him "no matter what,"

106

you have begun to solve your problem. But it is only the beginning; next follows an inventory of yourself and your marriage.

Take a long, hard look at yourself. After antagonisms have developed you cannot change your husband, nor can the preacher change him. The one person who can be changed is you. Take a look at your emotional life. Do you "fly off the handle" quickly, cry unnecessarily, talk compulsively? Are you moody or easily depressed? Take a look at your social life. Is it interfering with your family? Do your friends contribute to or destroy your home? Are you entertaining, attractive? Or dull, boorish, embarrassing?

Your spiritual life should come in for examination. Do the fruits of the spirit—love, joy, peace, patience, and the like—dominate your life? Would any man look at you twice because of the way you dress in your husband's presence? If not, why should your mate?

Then take a look at what you do to your husband. When he tries to help with the dishes, do you make him feel like a clumsy ox? When he tries to tell a story, do you treat him like a liar or an idiot? When he tries to work around the house, do you make him feel that he is inferior to other men? Is he simply another child to be corrected or developed? If so, then it is no wonder that he falls for the woman who makes him feel that he is generous, intelligent, and helpful.

It would be helpful also to take a look at what you let him do for you. We love people who bring out the best in us and no man can be drawn to a woman unless he feels that he is doing something fine and noble, something exciting and tender, something good for her. The girl who

107

has won him is probably not as able as you are. In all likelihood she is a person who has had troubles and your husband has come to her as an advisor. He has given her strength to face her problems and has shown her love. When a man does that for a woman he is likely to feel that he is in love with her. He becomes her "knight in shining armor."

When a couple gets married it is usually because they would rather go to dinner with each other, dance with each other, play tennis with each other, talk with each other, study with each other than with anyone else in the world. After marriage, some people begin to do things separately. The girl who goes to baseball games with her fiance and then is not interested in baseball after marriage, is asking for trouble. If a couple have allowed their activities together to be limited to eating breakfast and sleeping, then their marriage is on dangerous ground.

Finally, you should look at the externals of marriage. Family, finances, and friends can be the allies or the enemies of good marriages. Couples who allow them to get out of control are inviting destruction.

Maintaining the Christian concept of permanence in marriage, maintaining your love even after your marriage partner becomes an enemy, fulfilling the responsibilities of marriage after the luster is gone, taking an honest look at yourself and your marriage—all this requires a spiritual strength and poise that can come only in the most mature Christian life. It requires faith in the God who can see you through every dark valley of life. It requires an ability to forgive which is present only in the person who knows that he has been forgiven. It requires the fruits of the spirit of which Paul speaks: ". . . the fruit of the Spirit is

love, joy, peace, patience, kindness, goodness, faithful-
ness, gentleness, self-control; against such there is no law"
(GALATIANS 5:22-23).

One woman who had gone through the experience of
separation said, "I am sorry that he left me. I hope I can
get him back. But I would not give up the spiritual growth
that has taken place during this experience—even to get
my husband back." Your tragedy can be the open door
to your greatest triumph if you allow the God and Father
of our Lord Jesus Christ to walk with you through it.

11

your heart's desire

"*YOU SHALL* not covet your neighbor's house; you shall not covet your neighbor's wife, or his manservant, or his maidservant, or his ox, or his ass, or anything that is your neighbor's" (EXODUS 20:17).

The Hungarians wanted to run their own country but Russia wanted to run Hungary. The Hungarians revolted and Russia sent in tanks. Now hundreds are dead and thousands are refugees because two nations tried to govern one piece of territory.

The woman was in tears. She was in love but the other woman loved her husband and would not give him a divorce. Three children, two women, one man, and scores of friends were unhappy, and some of their lives were ruined, because two women wanted one man.

The king saw a beautiful vineyard; it was just what he wanted. When he tried to buy it, Naboth, the owner, would not sell. The queen heard about her husband's unhappiness and arranged for Naboth to be murdered. Then she presented the property to her husband. One man was killed because two men wanted the same piece of property.

Abraham Lincoln was watching his two boys fight. When someone asked him what was the trouble, Lincoln

110

replied, "Just what's the matter with the whole world. They've got three walnuts and each of them wants two."

Trouble begins when two nations try to rule one land, two women try to marry one man, two men try to own one farm, or two boys try to divide three walnuts.

The Bible describes our problem in this way: "What causes wars, and what causes fightings among you? Is it not your passions that are at war in your members? You desire and do not have; so you kill. And you covet and cannot obtain; so you fight and wage war" (JAMES 4:1-2). From the time Eve wanted the forbidden fruit, man's desires have been the roots of war, murder, rape, theft, deception, and false witnessing.

Some say that desire is only a problem for those who do not get what they want. Eve had no problem with her desires; she took the fruit. David had no problem with his love; he took Bathsheba. Ahab had no problem with the vineyard; Jezebel took it for him. Alexander had no problem with the world; he conquered it. Hitler had no problem with the Jews; he killed them.

It does seem at first glance that only the weak have problems and that the strong get what they want. Of course this does not seem fair, but what place has fairness or justice in the code of those who take what they want?

Man has long sought to solve the problems caused by his desires. Some ancient Babylonians said, "Let's pass a law," and they did—so did a lot of other people for many generations. But the camels still broke the Damascus speed limit and liquor still flowed. Apparently laws were all right for people who didn't desire to break them. As for the others, well, passing a law against something only seemed to make them want it more.

111

Once there was a man who proclaimed that he had discovered a magic formula for turning soapsuds into gold. He whipped up a tubful of suds, set it in the public square, and offered it at a trifling fee (for even magicians must live) to anyone who would follow his instructions for turning it into gold. To each applicant, after cannily taking his fee, he gave a wooden paddle and the simple directions: stir for one hour clockwise, and one hour counter-clockwise; but during those two hours you must not think of any white horse. He repeated the directions several times, emphasizing the importance of not thinking about the white horse. One fleeting thought of such an animal would break the spell and the soapsuds would not change into gold.

"So one applicant after another tried and failed. It was that wretched horse; he would come into their minds, try as they might to keep him out. At last the citizens lynched the magician, for they felt . . . that it was his magic that popped that horse into the mind of everyone who stirred the soapsuds."

Suggesting that people should not do something does not prevent them from doing it, unless of course they do not have the power to override the police. Of course this is an extreme attitude but it has been the attitude of nations in international coveting since the beginning of time. Laws can become scraps of paper and police forces can become tin soldiers in the paths of marching armies.

Somebody came up with another answer to the problem of desires and what to do about them: Instead of trying to enforce all these laws, why not produce everything that everyone wants? Why not give every family a money tree and put the latest Cadillac beside that brand-new Continental in every garage? That was a little impractical—there wasn't enough of anything to fill that much desire!

The Communists believe that if everyone shares in the economy everyone will have something, even if it isn't exactly what he wants. That's the way they are trying to solve the problem of desire. But many wives did not keep David from wanting Bathsheba; many fruit trees did not keep Eve from wanting the forbidden fruit; many vineyards did not keep Ahab from wanting another man's property.

A variation of this system was tried by several monastic orders of the church. The members of these orders took vows of poverty when they entered the monasteries, but it was only a matter of time before the monasteries became the owners of all the land surrounding them. Thus, while some men may sublimate their covetousness as individuals, they eventually express it through the group.

Eventually man turned to his religion for a solution to the problem of two people who want one thing, one space, one person, one reputation, or one job. In the Far East, Hindus felt that desires, when expressed, led to social difficulties; when repressed, they led to frustration. They decided to do away with all frustration by doing away with all desire. Some people have thought that this represented the Christian ethic and they have quoted the Apostle Paul: ". . . I have learned, in whatever state I am, to be content" (PHILIPPIANS 4:11). They have also quoted Jesus: ". . . life is more than food, and the body more than clothing" (LUKE 12:23).

The most serious difficulty about this view is that progress is made only by people who want something. It is only when people desperately desire good health that medical progress is made; only as they want to overcome harsh working conditions that machines are invented; only as they want to overcome the misfortunes of drought and flood that dams are built. Some of mankind's problems would be solved even if people wanted nothing, but men would cease to be the creatures that God made them. They would be selfish, callous, hardened beasts who had no concern for the sick, the needy, or the oppressed.

The tenth commandment is not opposed to desire. Some people have an idea that this commandment says only, "Neither shall you covet . . ." (DEUTERONOMY 5:21), but that is only part of it. Nowhere in Scripture is there any indication that a man should try to destroy his desires. The word that we translate "covet" in this commandment is usually translated "desire." In speaking of the commandments the Psalmist says, "More to be desired are they than gold, even much fine gold" (PSALMS 19:10). One of the most pitiful epitaphs ever written described a king of Jerusalem: he "departed without being desired" (II CHRONICLES 21:20, KJV), or as the Revised Standard Version translates it: ". . . he departed with no one's regret." To desire and to be desired is not considered wrong.

God has made us so that we do have desire. What is forbidden is not the desire for a wife but the desire for a neighbor's wife. Similarly the Scriptures do not imply that a man should not want a house; it is the house belonging to one's neighbor that is not to be coveted.

Notice that the word used in the commandment is not "admire." There is no suggestion that a man should not

114

admire his neighbor's house, his wife, or his speed boat. At times he may admire them more than the owner does, for he does not have to worry about monthly payments.

One of the difficulties in modern marriage comes at this point. Before we marry we can simply enjoy admiring the other person; after we marry we must live with them. Bills, rearing the children, sickness, keeping up the house and yard, and planning supper do not enter into the premarital way of living, but after marriage these problems do at times blind our eyes to the admiration we once held for our partner.

Kenneth Foreman says, "Coveting is not the same thing as admiring; and admiration need not be a sin. I can admire a sunset without wanting to own it or to take it away from anyone. So I can admire my neighbor's house or my neighbor's wife without wanting either one. Admiration is of the nature of aesthetic enjoyment, and that kind of pleasure differs from other kinds in being impersonal, quite different from the pleasure of ownership or control. . . . It is just the same, whether one is admiring a string of pearls in the jeweler's window, or on a neighbor's throat, or seeing it in the mirror on one's own."

The Hebrew answer to the problem of man's desire is not to do away with it, or with admiration, but to do away with the inner desire that would cut across a neighbor's rights. The Hebrews advocate an orientation of values, with justice in first place. We may want something, but justice is to be desired more than gold—even much fine gold.

In Christ there is a transforming power which "makes us love everybody." Christ met the old problem of coveting a neighbor's wife or his house by making a man love

115

his neighbor. The minute you love a neighbor you cease to want to hurt him.

I shall never forget an experience I once had. The woman was crying. She was single and wanted to be married. She had fallen in love with a man, and he with her, but he was already married and had children. I talked to both of them a number of times. Finally, I got the woman to agree to try to make friends with the wife of the man. At the same time she agreed to read the Bible, have regular prayer, attend church, and go out with other persons. She was not to see the man alone during this period.

At first she despised the man's wife, but as she saw more of her she came to like her. It was a difficult road with many setbacks but finally her admiration for the wife and her love for the children took away her passion to take a husband and father away from his family. In the course of the treatment, the woman got rid of some of her tension, gave up her clandestine meetings, found inner peace, and finally fell in love with a man who was free to marry.

When the law of Christ's love is written in the heart of man, then man can control his desires so that they no longer destroy him and others. As Henry Sloan Coffin said, "Our safety from all . . . coveting lies in constantly looking off to Him, and letting Him draw out our every desire and confidence and fastening them on Himself."

As the church and its membership draw closer to Him, they can solve this problem of desire without social disruption or personal frustration. As we draw closer to Him, we will "covet earnestly the best gifts . . ." (1 CORINTHIANS 12:31, KJV), which Paul interprets as faith, hope, and love.

116

To a world terrified by the dangers of covetousness, the church offers Christ, the fairest of ten thousand. If He be lifted up He will draw all men unto Himself and away from themselves. From Christ we learn love. When we have love, we can take what we want.

12

the religious crisis
in our schools

THE SUPREME COURT of the United States recently handed down its decision that the recital of the Lord's Prayer and the reading of the Bible in public schools are unconstitutional. As was expected this brought about a reaction that has been notable for its heat and smoke but not for its light. The reaction comes from a recognition that this decision means the end of a tradition that has allied the Christian faith and the public-school system. Many Christians are fearful of the consequences.

Our fears have been best expressed in an article a century and a half old that I found in McGuffey's *Fifth Eclectic Reader,* which used to be a classic textbook of our primary schools:

> And, let men thoroughly believe that they are the work and sport of chance; that no superior intelligence concerns itself with human affairs; that all their improvements perish forever at death; that the weak have no guardian, and the injured no avenger; that there is no recompense for sacrifices to uprightness and the public good;

118

that an oath is unheard in heaven; that secret crimes have no witness but the perpetrator; that human existence has no purpose, and human virtue no unfailing friend; that this brief life is everything to us, and death is total, everlasting extinction; once let them thoroughly abandon religion, and who can conceive or describe the extent of the desolation which would follow?

We hope, perhaps, that human laws and natural sympathy would hold society together. As reasonably might we believe that were the sun quenched in the heavens, our torches would illuminate, and our fires quicken and fertilize the creation. What is there in human nature to awaken respect and tenderness, if man is the unprotected insect of a day? And what is he more, if atheism be true?

Erase all thought and fear of God from a community, and selfishness and sensuality would absorb the whole man. Appetite, knowing no restraint, and suffering, having no solace or hope, would trample in scorn on the restraints of human laws. Virtue, duty, principle, would be mocked and spurned as unmeaning sounds. A sordid self-interest would supplant every feeling; and man would become, in fact, what the theory in atheism declares him to be,—a companion for brutes.

The terrifying rise of delinquency in our major cities is ample evidence of the failure of our educational system to teach children about God or about what God requires of man. A continuation of our present system will lead only to increased juvenile gang wars, increased thefts, rapes, and a continued debasement of the values upon which our democratic society is built.

While I am convinced that most of our alarm at the decision of the Supreme Court arises from fears such as those suggested above, we must be honest and admit that some of our reaction arises from our dislike of those living close to us who are different from us in religion or culture. There still remains a wall of misunderstanding between Protestants, Roman Catholics, and Jews. When you add to this our feeling that we Protestants are being pushed around after having controlled the public schools since their beginning, it is not hard to understand why there is so much heat and smoke and so little light.

Is there any Word from God to guide us toward a solution of our problem? It seems to me that two Words are particularly pertinent here. The first is found in the Book of Deuteronomy and has been the foundation of Judaism's survival through the centuries even though its children have attended schools of those who had a different religion:

> "Hear, O Israel: The Lord our God is one Lord; and you shall love the Lord your God with all your heart, and with all your soul, and with all your might. And these words which I command you this day shall be upon your heart; and you shall teach them diligently to your children, and shall talk of them when you sit in your house, and when you walk by the way, and when you lie down, and when you rise. And you

120

shall bind them as a sign upon your hand, and
they shall be as frontlets between your eyes. And
you shall write them on the doorposts of your
house and on your gates" (DEUTERONOMY 6:4-9).

There are four fundamental requirements in this passage. First, we are to love God and obey His commandments. Second, we are to teach His Word and will to our
children. Third, we are to talk about Him to others.
Finally, we are to keep His Word and will in prominent
places in our lives.

Do you obey the Word of God? Do you observe the
Ten Commandments? Do your children know that you
obey these commandments? How much of the Bible have
you taught your family? It is a fine thing to want the
Bible taught in the schools, but the place where it should
be taught is in the home.

Do your children know the Books of the Bible, the Ten
Commandments, the Twenty-third Psalm, the Lord's
Prayer, the Sermon on the Mount? If in your home you
do not have a blessing before meals you should not utter
pious objections because your children are not allowed to
say the Lord's Prayer in public school. Ask first if you
have ruled out God in your home. Why pluck the mote
out of the Supreme Court's eyes if you have a beam in
your own eyes?

We Christians have another arm of religious education
—the church. The most bitter and vitriolic battles between
religion and education are not being fought now; they
were at their height in the first half of the nineteenth
century. From 1820 to 1850 they were particularly emotional in New England, and during this same period the

church school had its beginning and first great development in this country. The impetus for the establishment of a church education program came from the reaction to the efforts to push religion out of the public schools 150 years ago.

Since that time the church school has continued to grow. In the period since 1926, while the national population has grown 53 per cent, our church-school enrollment has increased 90 per cent. At its height in 1959, Protestant church-school enrollment included 22.7 per cent of our total American population. In addition to our Sunday morning church schools, we Christians have vacation church schools, youth weeks, and summer camping programs, so it can be seen that the church has not been asleep while religion has been removed from the public schools.

The recent decision of our Supreme Court makes almost final what began over 150 years ago. It should give new and greater stimulus to the movements of Protestants, Catholics, and Jews to strengthen their programs of education.

In the Protestant churches this should be done in three areas. First, we must have the best curriculum possible. I believe that almost all of our churches have completely revised their educational programs in the past few years. Second, we need better-trained teachers. Third, and most important, we must reach out.

While 41.8 per cent of all primary school children in our country are enrolled in Protestant church schools, 58.2 per cent are not. Are your neighbors' children attending a church school? Their lack of faith will keep your children from being interested in attending. Their delinquency will influence your child. Have you attempted to get them enrolled?

Even more serious is the fact that only 23.1 per cent of our junior- and senior-high young people are enrolled in Christian education programs. This means that 76.9 per cent of our youth are not enrolled. Have you thought of filling up your car with teen-agers and bringing them to Sunday school, or are you content just to send your own child?

There is a second Word from God that relates to our problem, and it comes from the teaching of our Lord. He told His disciples: " 'Behold, I send you out as sheep in the midst of wolves; so be wise as serpents and innocent as doves' " (MATTHEW 10:16). The obvious meaning here is usually overlooked. We might put it differently today and say that we should keep our own skirts clean.

A noted churchman has said of the Supreme Court decision that "It can only mean that our American heritage is being abandoned in imitation of Soviet philosophy, of Soviet materialism and of Soviet regimented liberty." Fortunately, many people would not agree with him.

There is a tremendous difference between Soviet education and our own. Soviet education is atheistic in the sense that it denounces and ridicules religion. One of its fundamental purposes is to eradicate religion. Our Supreme Court has not sponsored or advocated such a policy. It is one thing for you to keep silent about me and quite another for you to lie about me because you want to destroy me. Neutrality is not the equivalent of antagonism, and in our concern we must be sure that we are honest and are not simply calling names. While there is no command from God that says we should teach religion in our public schools, there is a command that says we should not bear false witness. To be ignorant about the decision of our Supreme Court, or to mislead and thus create unwarranted division in our land, is inexcusable.

We must also be innocent of hypocrisy. I must admit that I have grown tired of hearing those Protestants who talk so much about separation of church and state and yet would make the public schools the educational arm of the Protestant Church. Let it be admitted that the chief purpose of the colonial public schools was to teach reading, the Psalms, the Lord's Prayer, and the catechism. Let us also admit that they did not talk about the separation of church and state at the same time.

I am equally disgusted by Roman Catholics who make much of the rights of minorities and yet support a church that allows no freedom of expression in Spain or Latin America. I have this same feeling about our Jewish friends who talk of civil liberties and yet support the country of Israel which requires the teaching of the Hebrew religion in its public schools.

To solve our problem we will have to be as innocent as doves. We must be honest in our speech and avoid the hypocrisy of wanting something for ourselves which we are not willing to grant to others.

Too many people think that innocence is enough, but indolent innocents can cause us to lose time and precious lives. They frequently are the dead weights that keep the church and most good movements from succeeding in our society.

The enemies of truth are the self-seekers who use pious phrases like "separation of church and state" and "Americanism" to cover their own selfish purposes, the rabble-rousers who use half-truths and whole falsehoods to divide our nation, and the indolent innocents who sit back while others do the thinking and the work.

Jesus said that while we keep ourselves innocent we are to be as wise as serpents. By this He meant that we are to use all just techniques to accomplish worthy goals.

I think that I can state my own goal rather simply. I believe that the fundamentals of religion and ethics should be taught in our public schools, but in such a way as to avoid infringements on the rights of others. The state must want our schools to turn out responsible as well as educated citizens. This cannot be done without some teaching of religion and ethics.

The Belgian government has met the problem by requiring all public-school children to take courses in either religion or ethics. The teachers of these courses must be approved by the educational accreditation boards as well as the various churches involved. Those students who wish to avoid religious courses must take courses in ethics. Thus the schools are making an attempt to turn out youths who are not only educated but responsible.

Another solution would be the development of more parochial schools. One factor that has hindered these schools in the past has been the cost involved. Many private schools have given up their religious orientation to become fashionable finishing schools for the children of the well-to-do, or specialized schools for the reformation of potential delinquents, or boarding houses for unwanted children.

A third approach to our problem is in the released-time concept that has already been approved by our Supreme

Court. We must wait to see the results of this experiment.

The weakness that marks much of our public-school system arises from our American cult of individuality. Failing to see that a lack of good education and responsible religious training among the children of the slums and children of minority groups would finally have destructive social effects, we have blindly sought good responsible education for our own children and left the rest to poor teachers, irresponsible ethics, and inadequate facilities. We are at last waking up to the dangers of such a system. The rising tide of juvenile delinquency and the tensions between majority and minority groups remind us that we can no longer afford the luxury of raising children without the sense of rightness and responsibility that comes from religion and ethics. We are living in a pluralistic society which demands equal justice in public institutions for all religious and ethical beliefs.

Unless we solve our problem in such a way as to raise responsible citizens, we can expect a continuation of juvenile delinquency, and the chaos that comes when these delinquents become adult destroyers. I do not believe that we are so overcome by hatred, or so blinded by prejudice and ignorance, that we cannot solve our problem. But it is going to take the most vigorous minds and concerted public action yet developed in our country during a time of peace. Where better can we start than right in our hometowns?

That means that you who are lawyers should seek to guide your neighbors into adequate solutions; you who are members of P.T.A. groups should discuss and study this problem; you who are parents should demand that something constructive be done; you who are involved in the news media should communicate the truth; you who are community leaders should try to work out adequate plans.

Every six-year delay will mean that another generation has gone through our primary schools without any adequate religious or ethical training. Time will not allow us to sit idly by while our society destroys itself. Can God, our youth, our church, and our society count on you to teach the Word of God to your own children, to bring unchurched children and youths to the church school, to use your influence to solve the problem which is at the root of our most humiliating national scandal?